Man, I Hate Cursive

Jim Benton

Andrews McMeel
Publishing®

a division of Andrews McMeel Universal

Other Books by Jim Benton

Dear Dumb Diary

Dog Butts and Love. And Stuff Like That. And Cats.

Franny K. Stein

It's Happy Bunny

Dedicated to Robert Benton,
who used to pull my crumpled-up drawings
out of the trash when I was a kid.

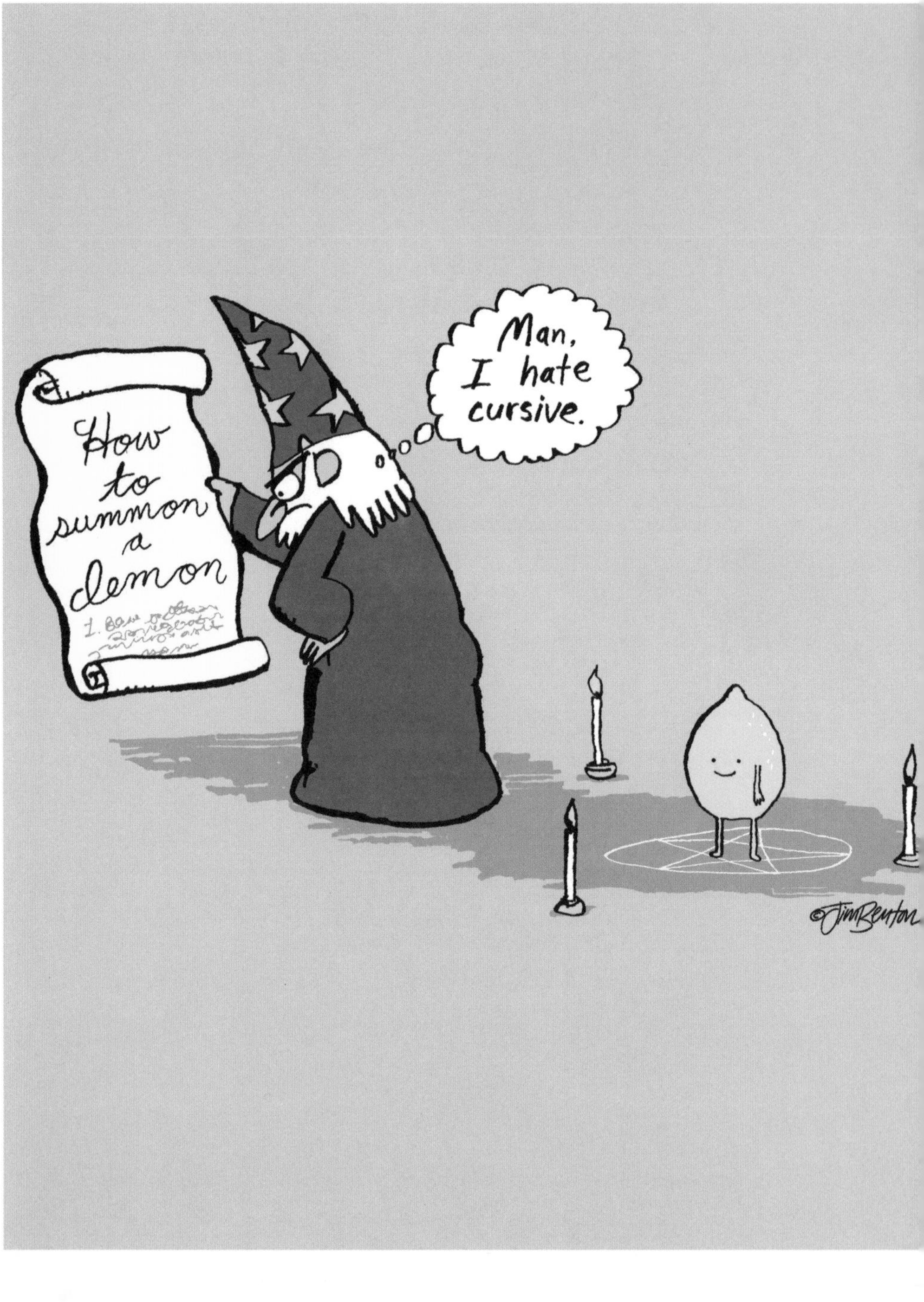
How to summon a demon
Man, I hate cursive.
©Jim Benton

How I got to Sleep.

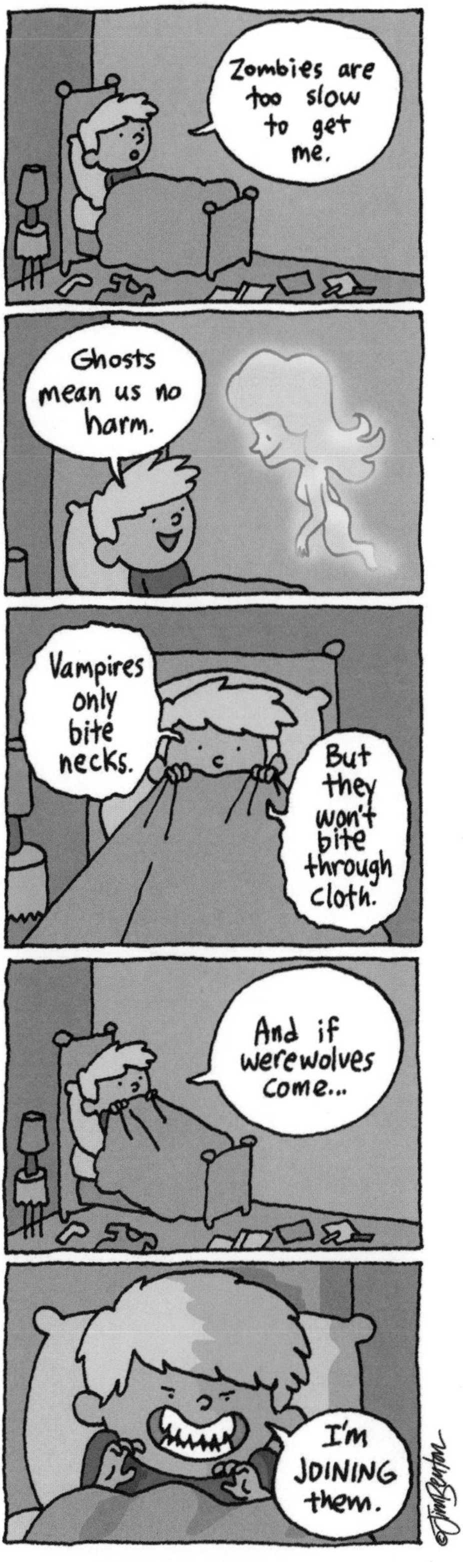
Zombies are too slow to get me.
Ghosts mean us no harm.
Vampires only bite necks.
But they won't bite through cloth.
And if werewolves come...
I'm JOINING them.

My Teachers

THE WHOLE WORLD IS MATH!
THE ENTIRE UNIVERSE IS CHEMISTRY!
THE VERY ESSENCE OF REALITY IS BEGINNER'S SPANISH!
©Jim Benton

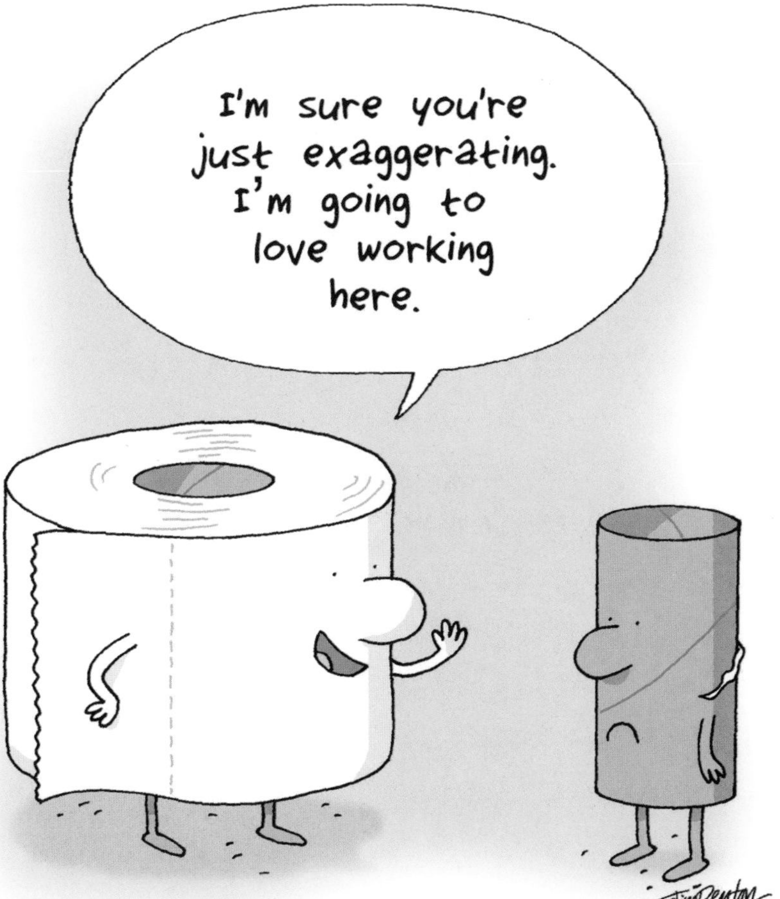
I'm sure you're just exaggerating. I'm going to love working here.
©Jim Benton

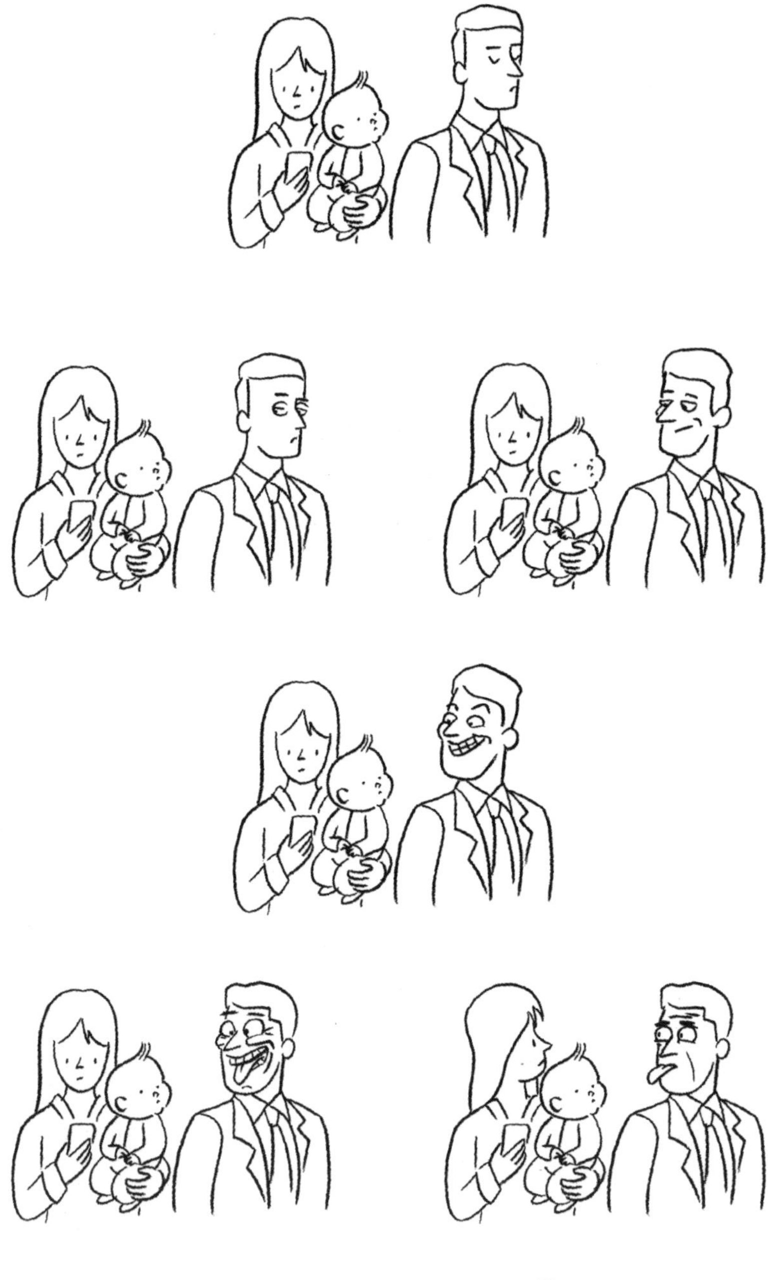
©Jim Benton

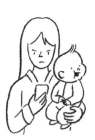

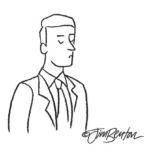

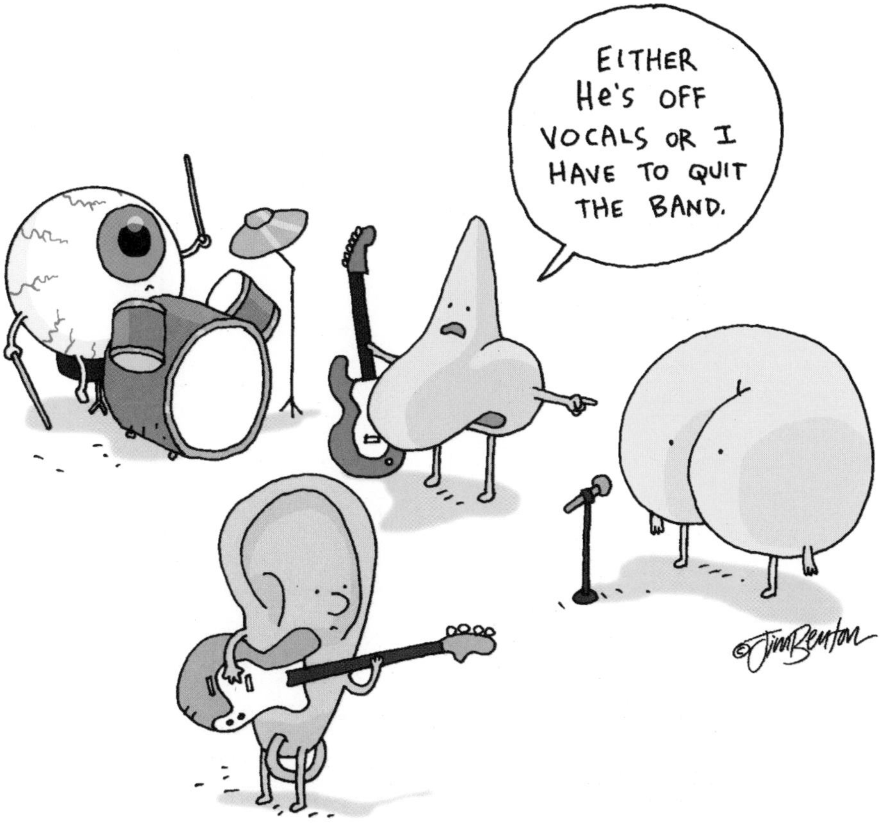
EITHER He's OFF VOCALS OR I HAVE TO QUIT THE BAND.
©Jim Benton

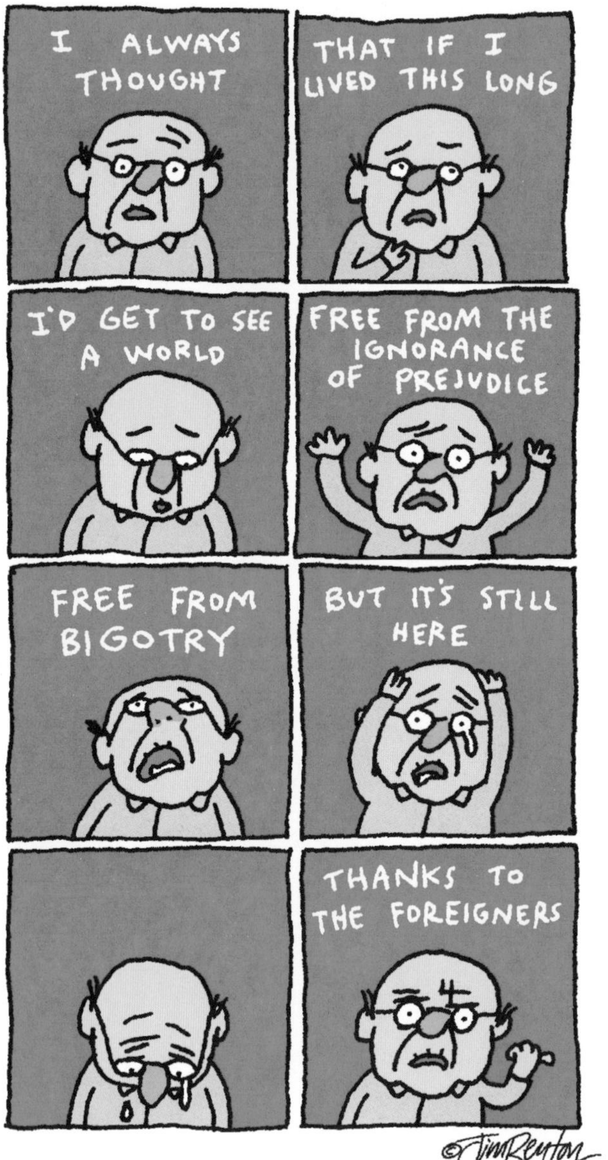
I ALWAYS THOUGHT
THAT IF I LIVED THIS LONG
I'D GET TO SEE A WORLD
FREE FROM THE IGNORANCE OF PREJUDICE
FREE FROM BIGOTRY
BUT IT'S STILL HERE
THANKS TO THE FOREIGNERS
©Jim Benton

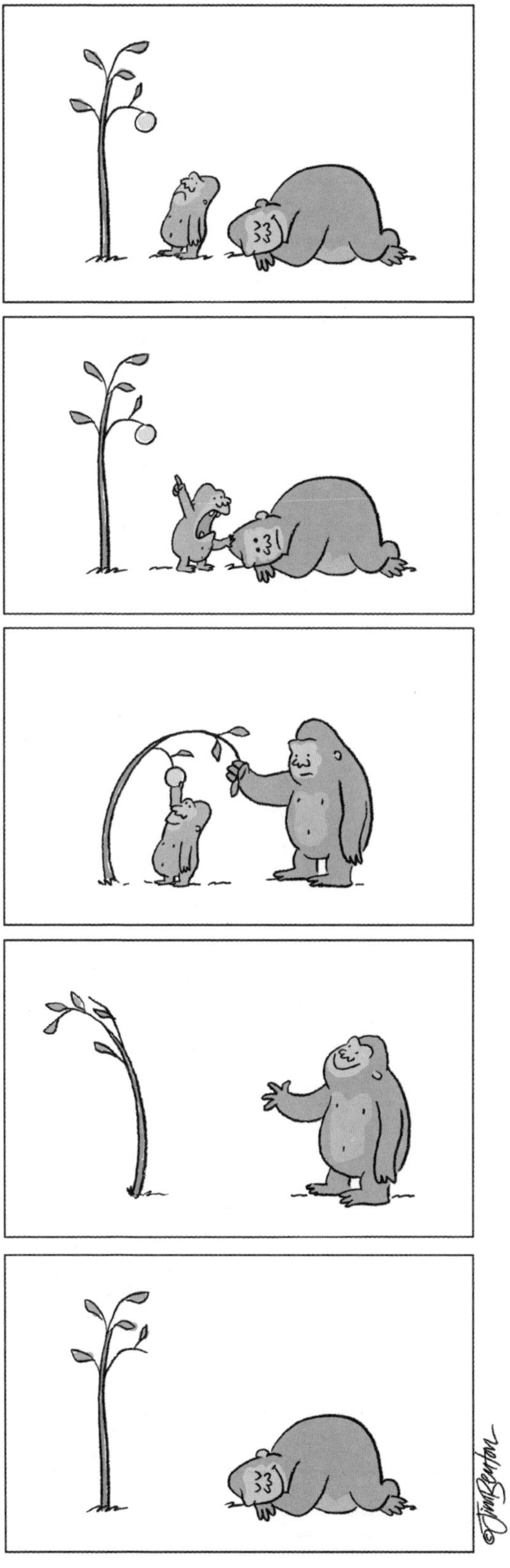
©Jim Benton

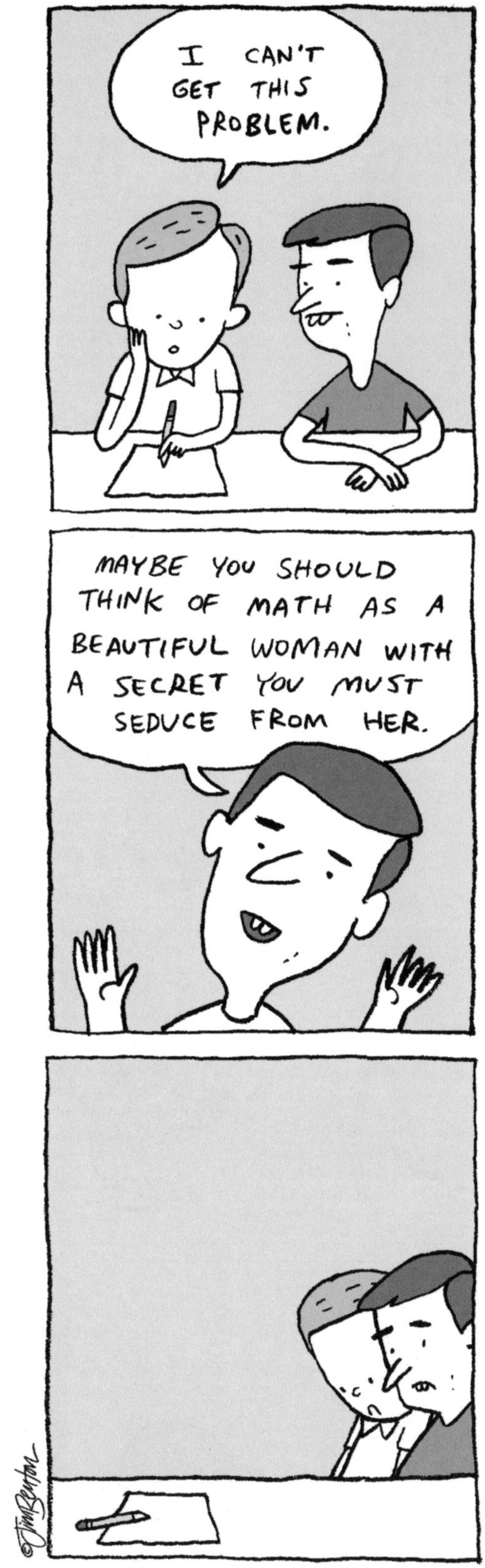
I CAN'T GET THIS PROBLEM.
MAYBE YOU SHOULD THINK OF MATH AS A BEAUTIFUL WOMAN WITH A SECRET YOU MUST SEDUCE FROM HER.
©Jim Benton

One day, her work will improve the lives of countless people.

But right now, she's in the next booth, and she is _too loud_.

Because she is currently a huge sillypants.

I think I can live with that.

©Jim Benton

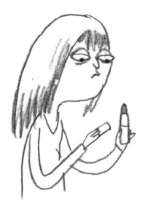

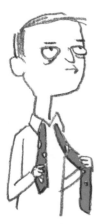

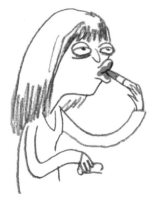

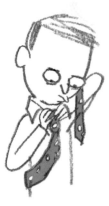

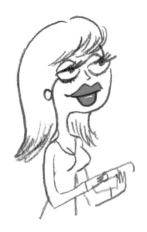

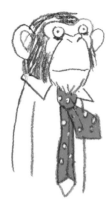

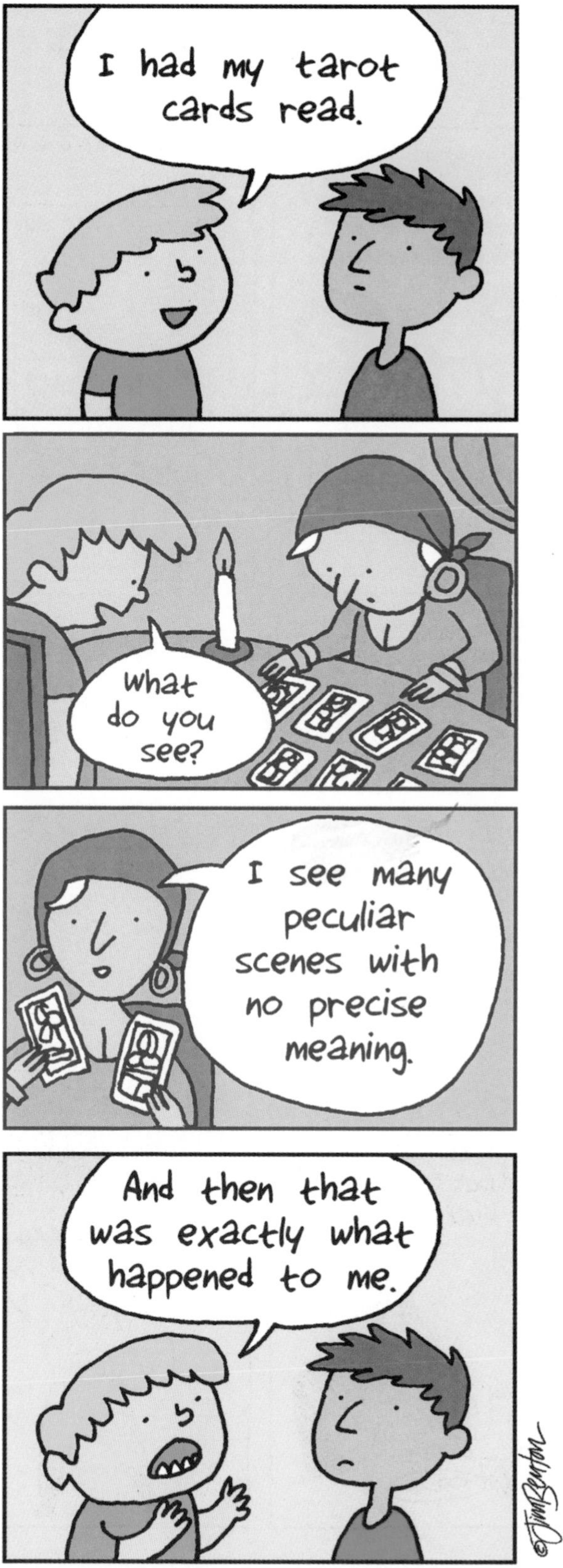
I had my tarot cards read.
what do you see?
I see many peculiar scenes with no precise meaning.
And then that was exactly what happened to me.
©Jim Benton

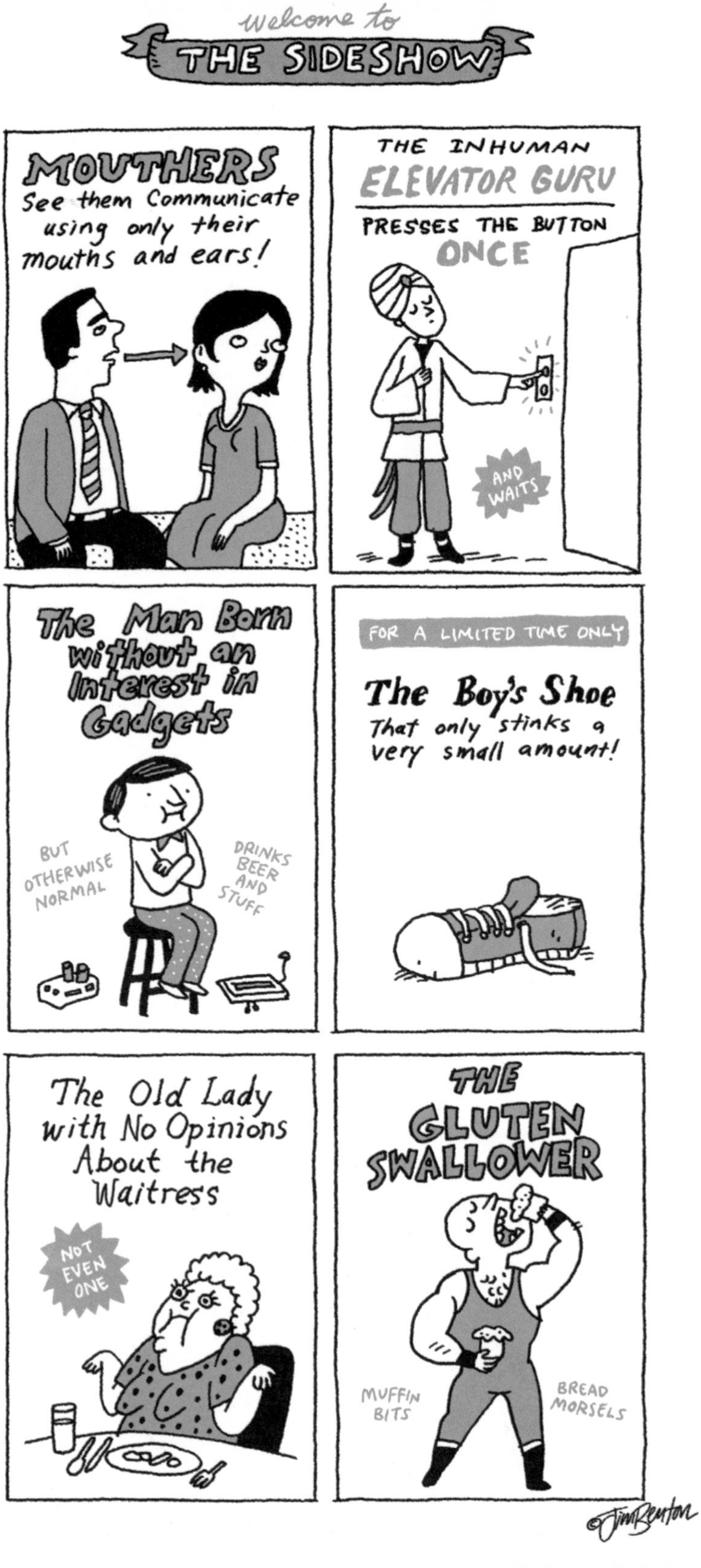
welcome to
THE SIDESHOW
MOUTHERS
See them Communicate using only their mouths and ears!
THE INHUMAN
ELEVATOR GURU
PRESSES THE BUTTON
ONCE
AND WAITS
The Man Born without an Interest in Gadgets
BUT OTHERWISE NORMAL
DRINKS BEER AND STUFF
FOR A LIMITED TIME ONLY
The Boy's Shoe
That only stinks a very small amount!
The Old Lady with No Opinions About the Waitress
NOT EVEN ONE
THE GLUTEN SWALLOWER
MUFFIN BITS
BREAD MORSELS
©Jim Benton

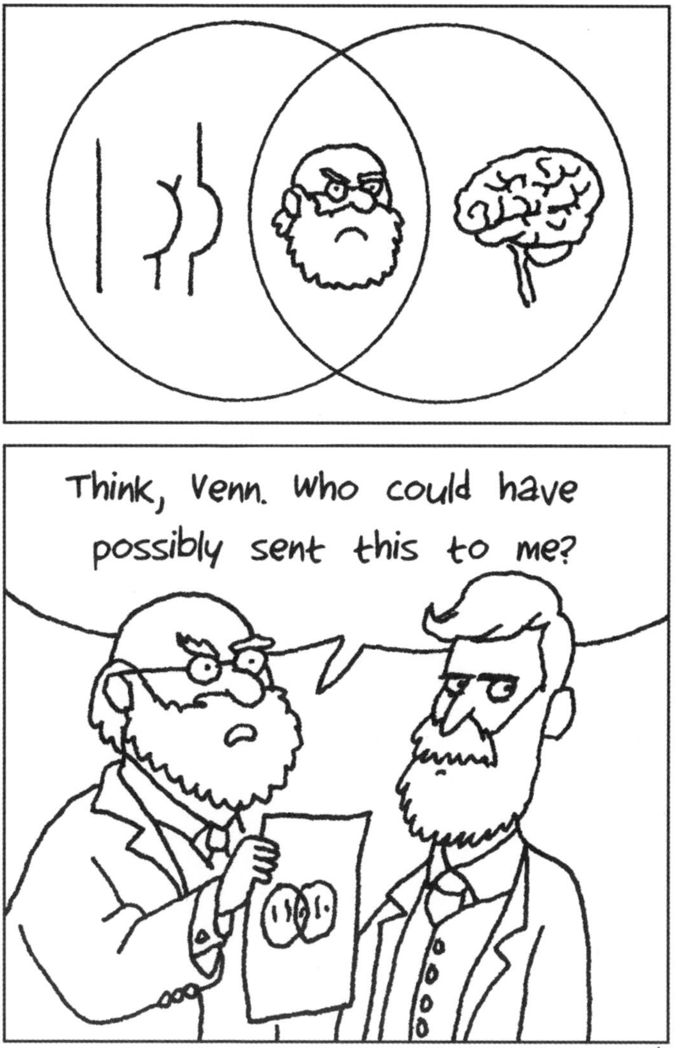
Think, Venn. Who could have possibly sent this to me?
©Jim Benton

©Jim Benton

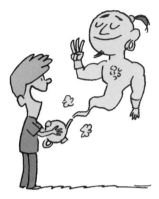

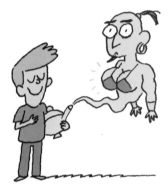

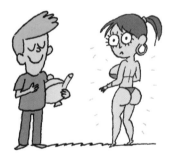

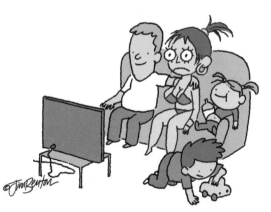

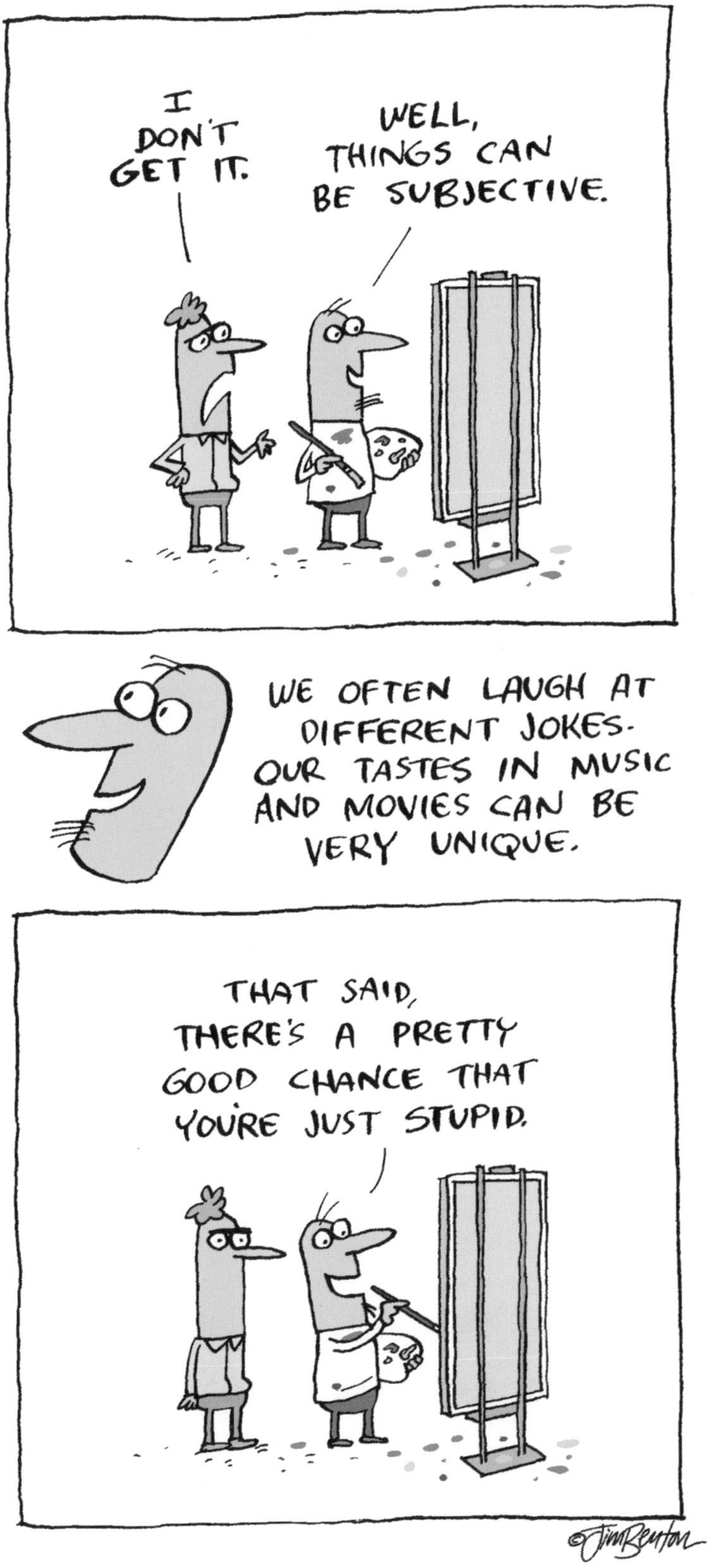
I DON'T GET IT.
WELL, THINGS CAN BE SUBJECTIVE.
WE OFTEN LAUGH AT DIFFERENT JOKES. OUR TASTES IN MUSIC AND MOVIES CAN BE VERY UNIQUE.
THAT SAID, THERE'S A PRETTY GOOD CHANCE THAT YOU'RE JUST STUPID.
©Jim Benton

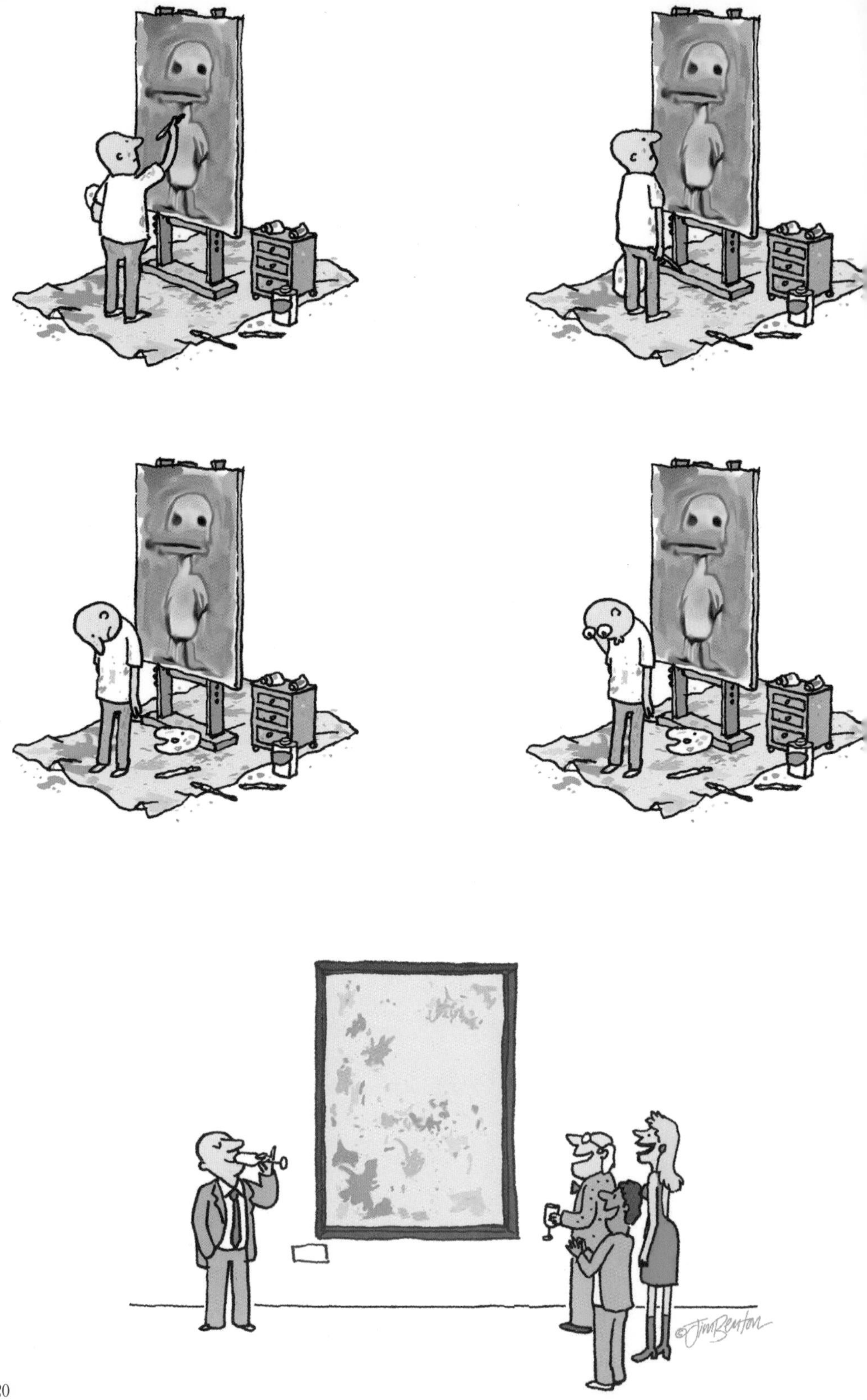
©Jim Benton

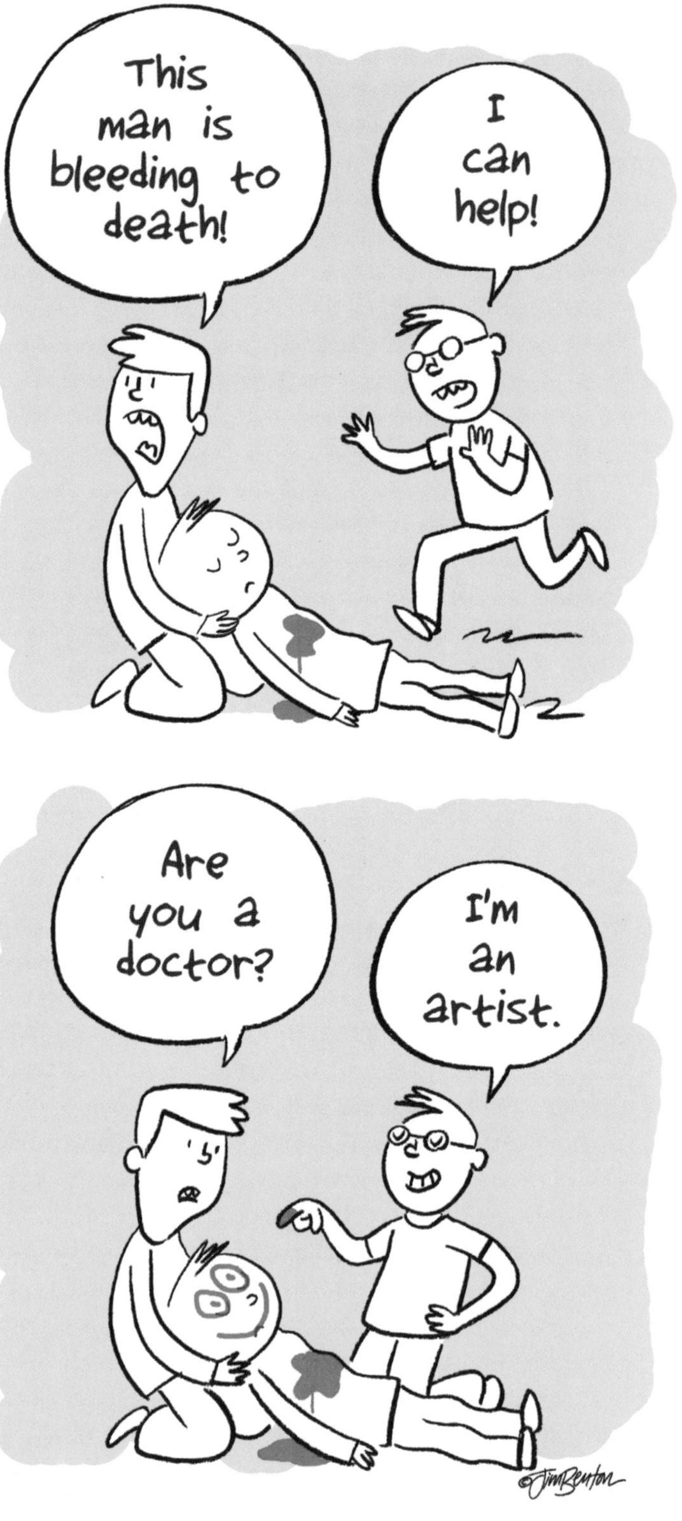
This man is bleeding to death!
I can help!
Are you a doctor?
I'm an artist.
©Jim Benton

"I'm looking for a computer with only bitter memory."

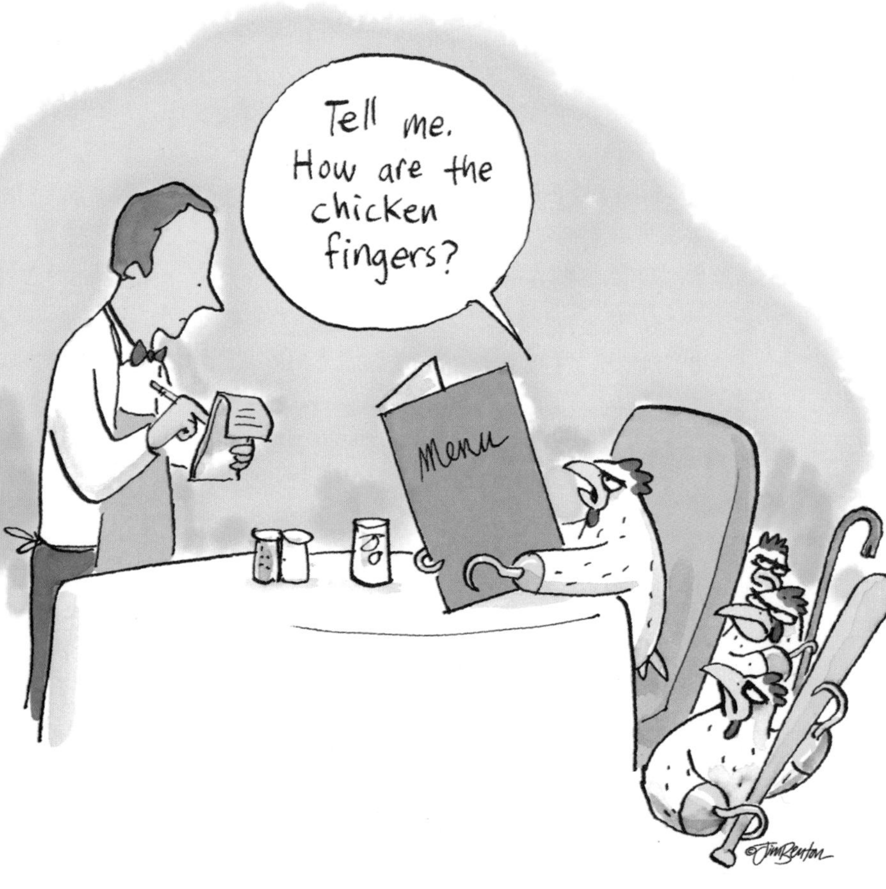
Tell me. How are the chicken fingers?
Menu
©JimBenton

"We should all be pretty darn proud that we had the integrity to steal a lot less than we could have."

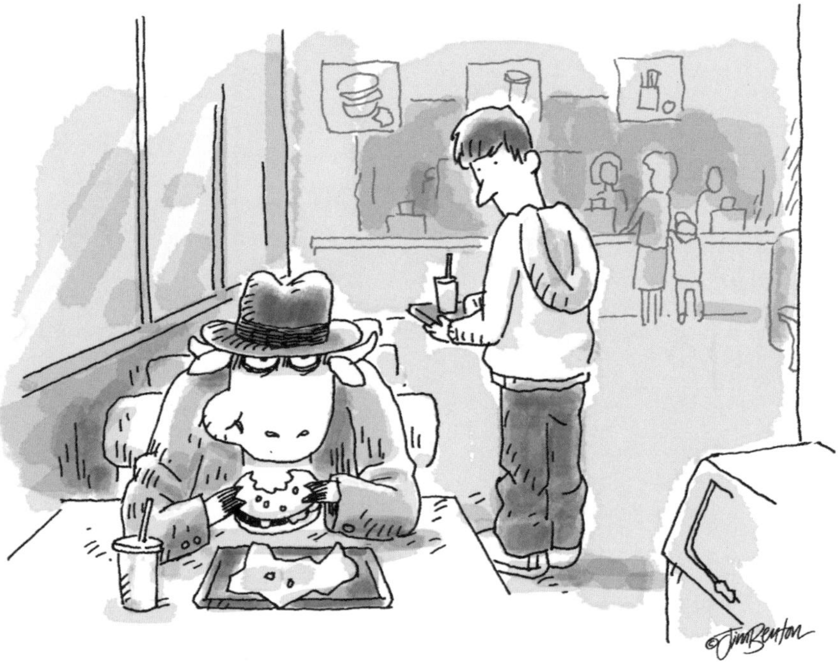
©Jim Benton

"Pretty good time to just keep on walking, son."

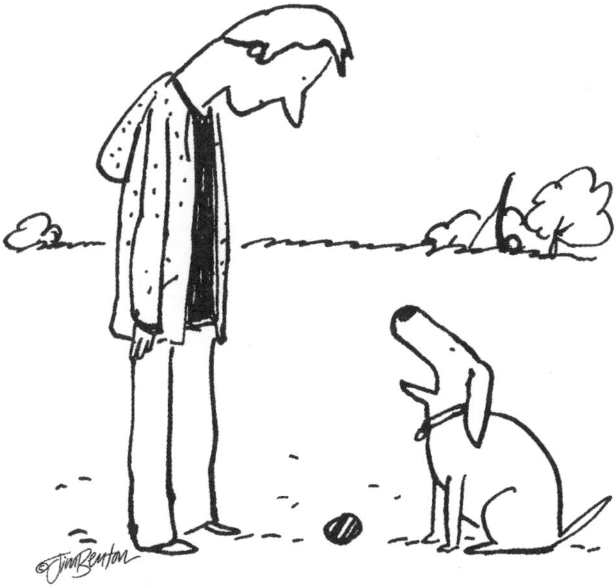
©Jim Benton

"You throw the ball, I bring it back.
You throw the ball, I bring it back.
I don't know who, but one of us is an asshole."

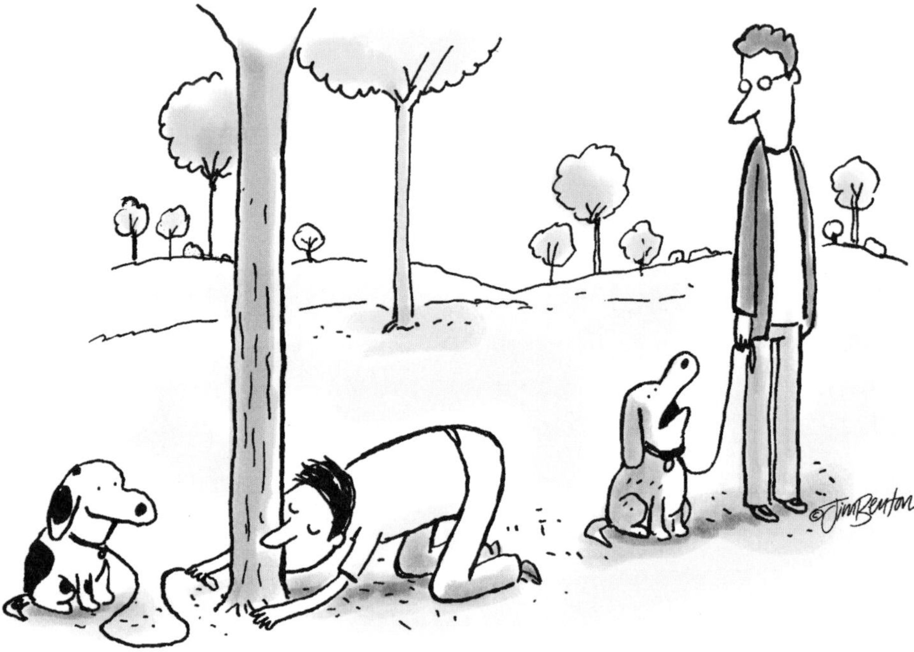
©Jim Benton

"It would be nice if you showed a little interest in ***my*** *work sometimes."*

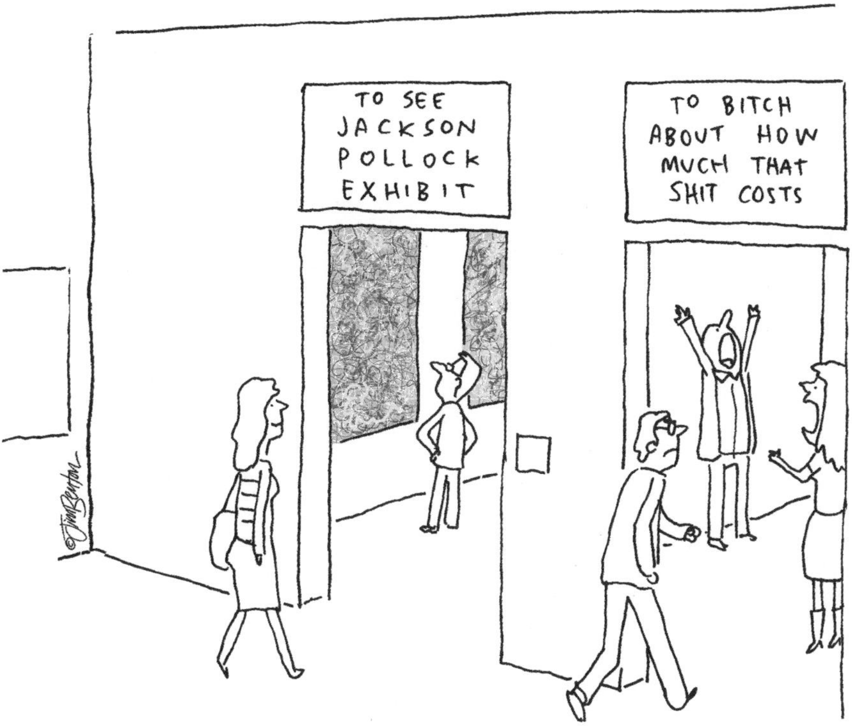
TO SEE JACKSON POLLOCK EXHIBIT
TO BITCH ABOUT HOW MUCH THAT SHIT COSTS

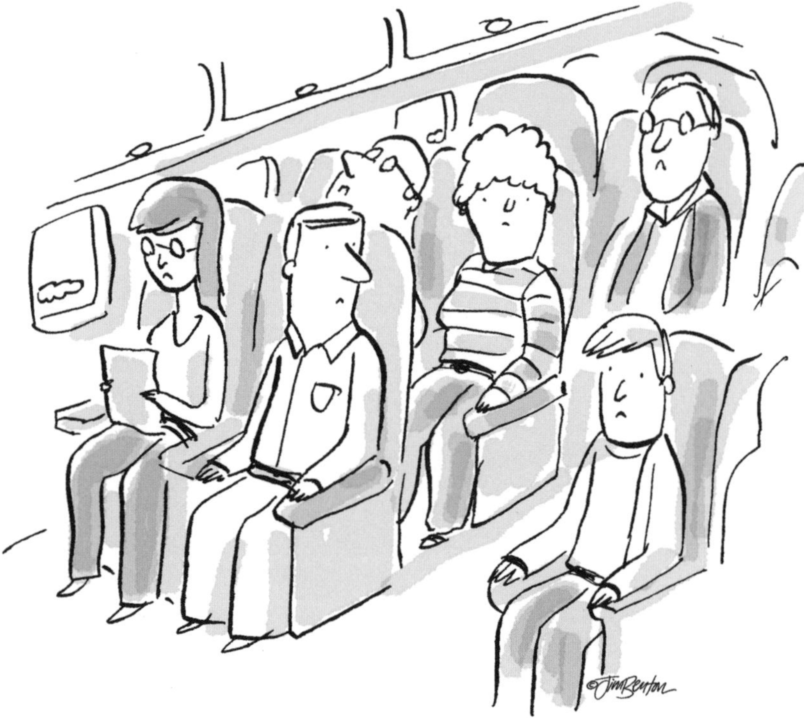
©Jim Benton

"This is the captain. Kind of a long shot, but did anybody bring some of that special airplane gasoline with them today?"

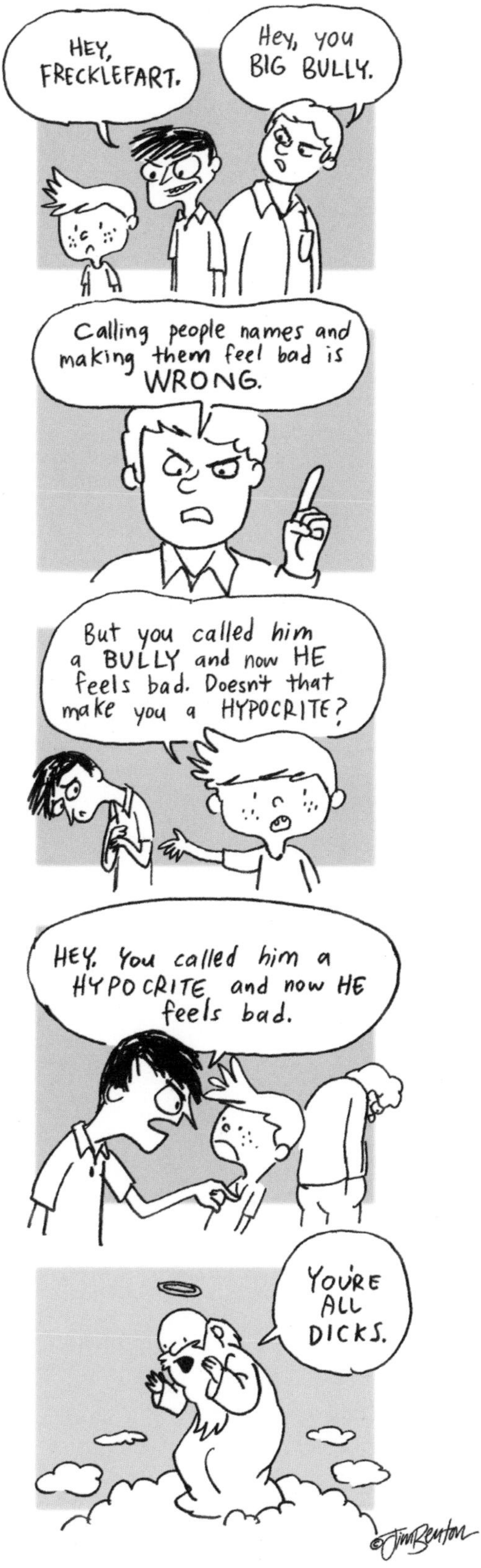
HEY, FRECKLEFART.
Hey, you BIG BULLY.
Calling people names and making them feel bad is WRONG.
But you called him a BULLY and now HE feels bad. Doesn't that make you a HYPOCRITE?
HEY. You called him a HYPOCRITE and now HE feels bad.
YOU'RE ALL DICKS.
©Jim Benton

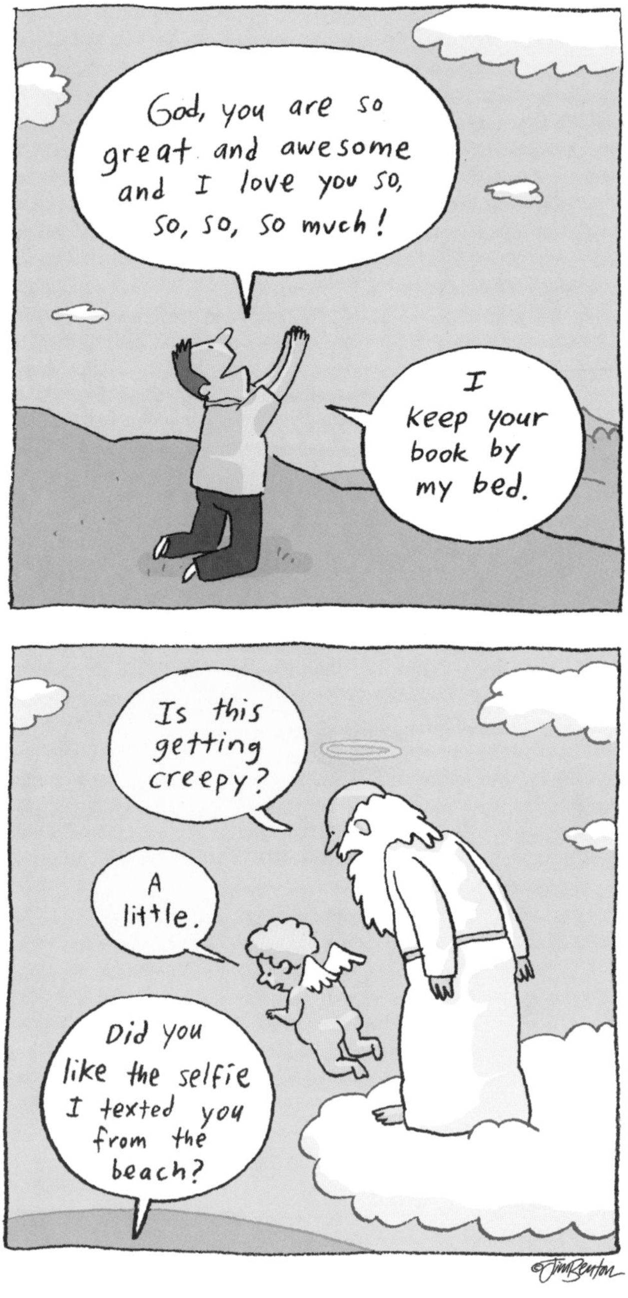
God, you are so great and awesome and I love you so, so, so, so much!
I keep your book by my bed.
Is this getting creepy?
A little.
Did you like the selfie I texted you from the beach?
©Jim Benton

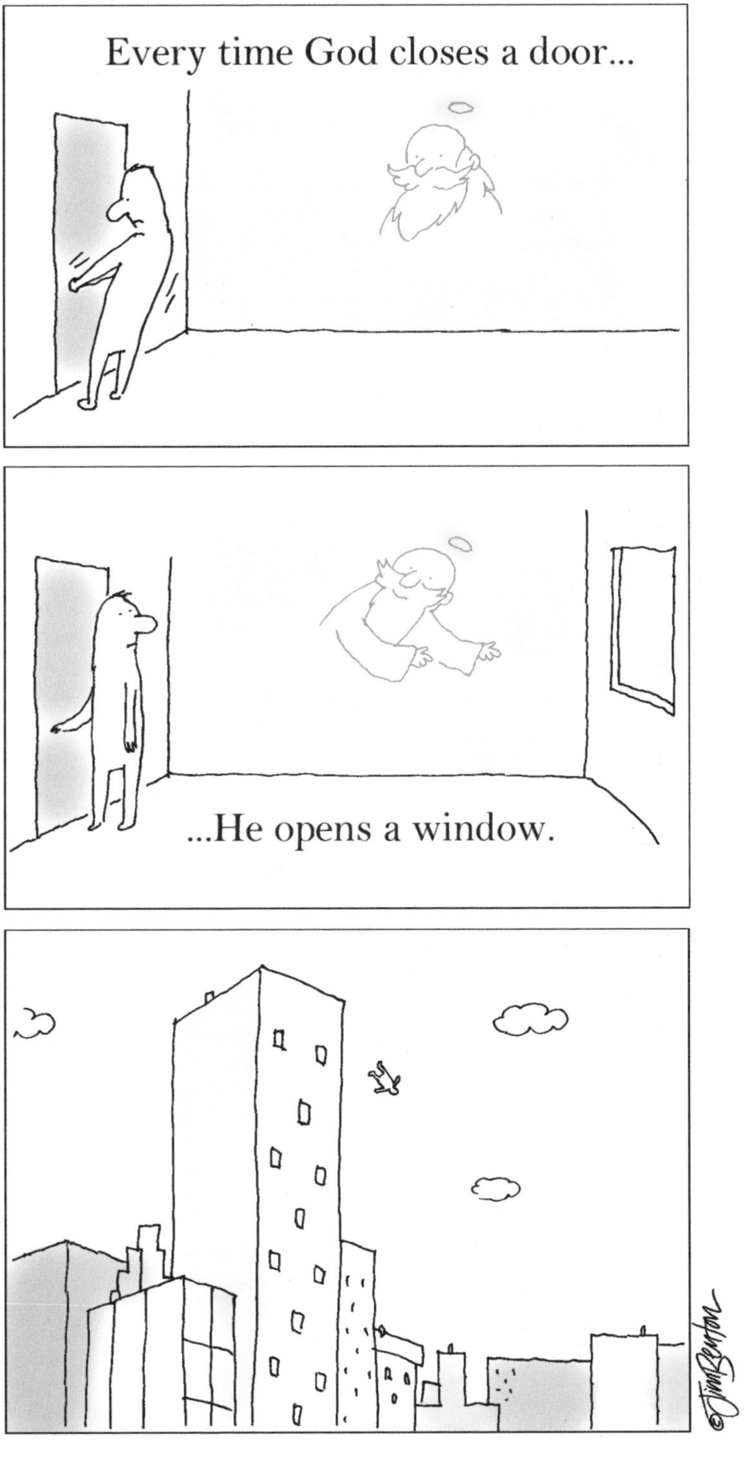
Every time God closes a door...
...He opens a window.

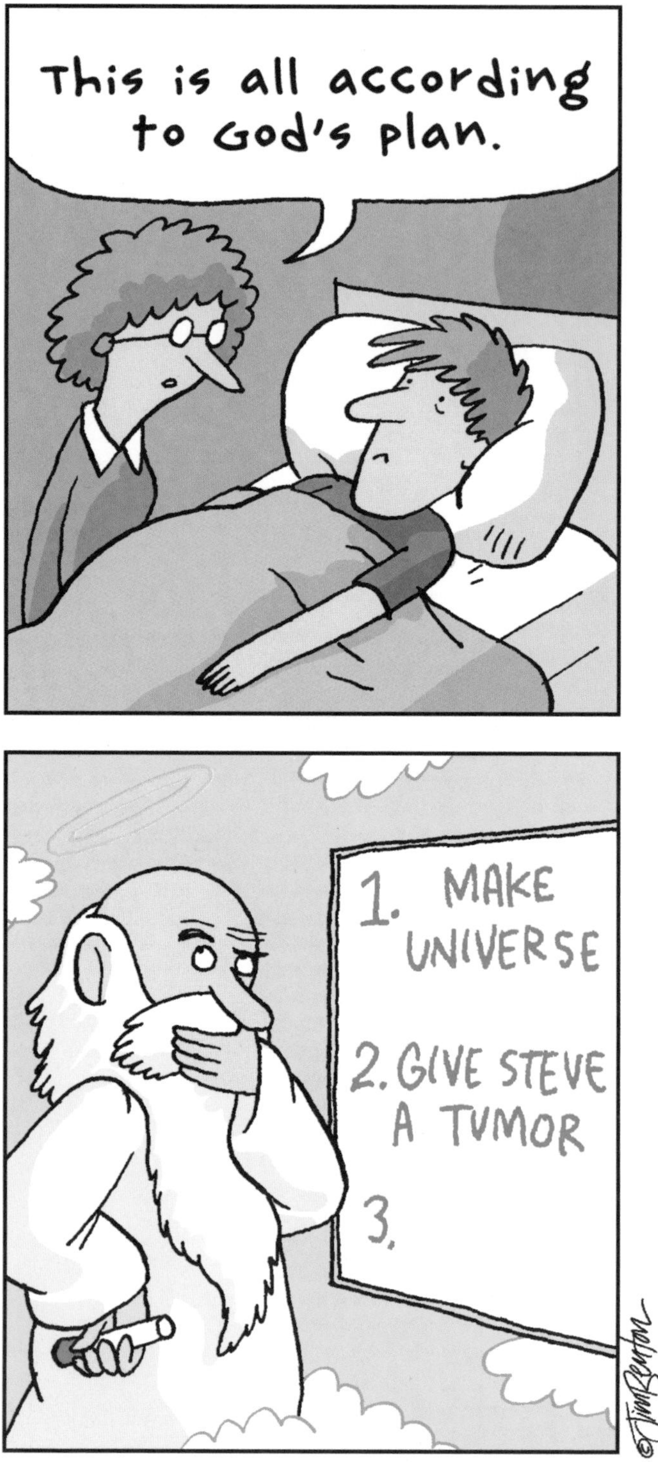
This is all according to God's plan.
1. MAKE UNIVERSE
2. GIVE STEVE A TUMOR
3.
©JimBenton

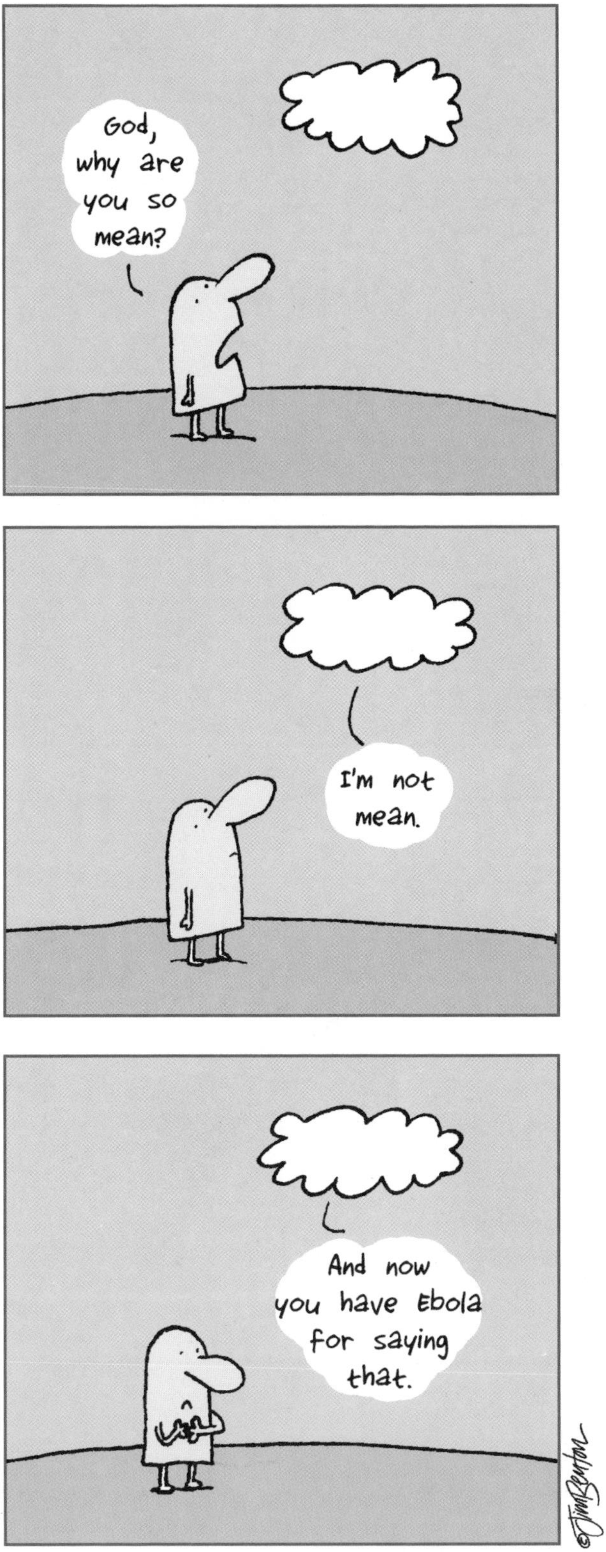
God, why are you so mean?
I'm not mean.
And now you have Ebola for saying that.

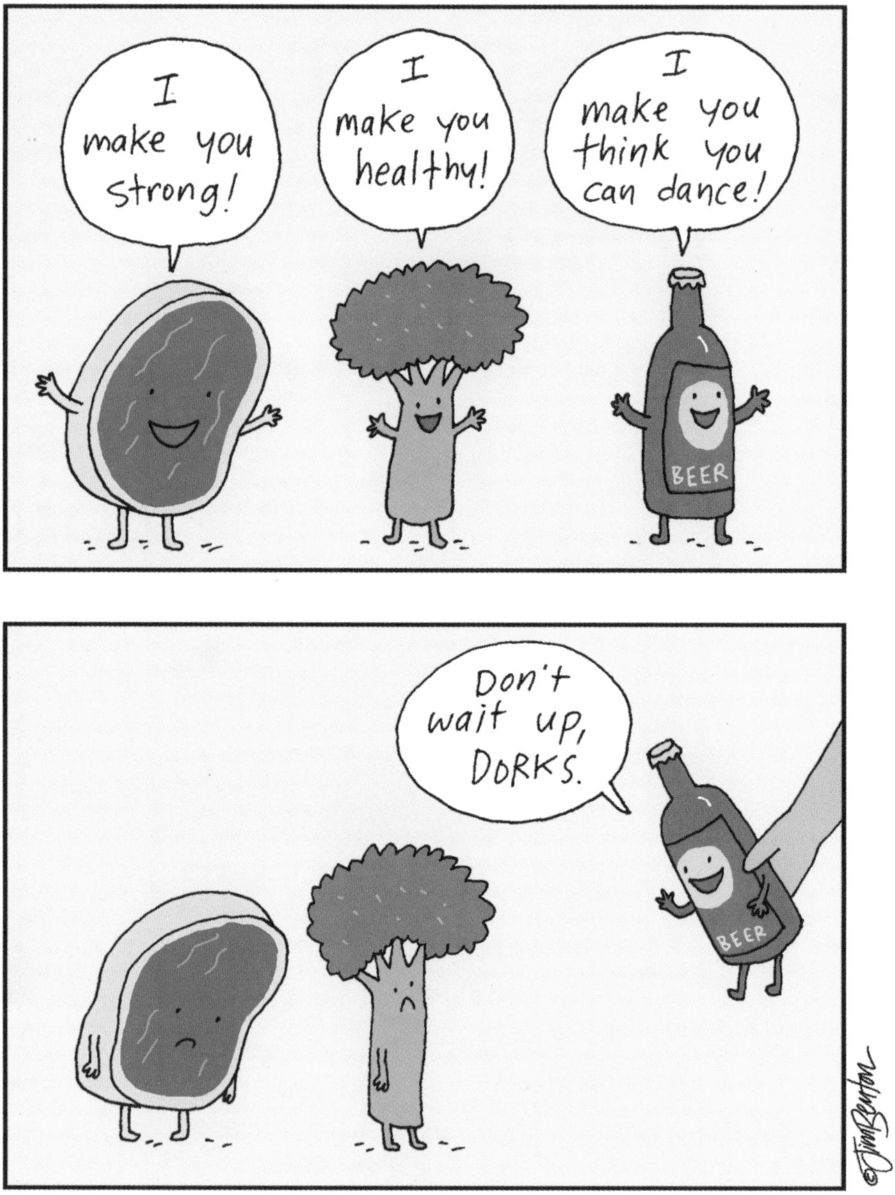
I make you strong!
I make you healthy!
I make you think you can dance!
BEER
Don't wait up, DORKS.
BEER
©Jim Benton

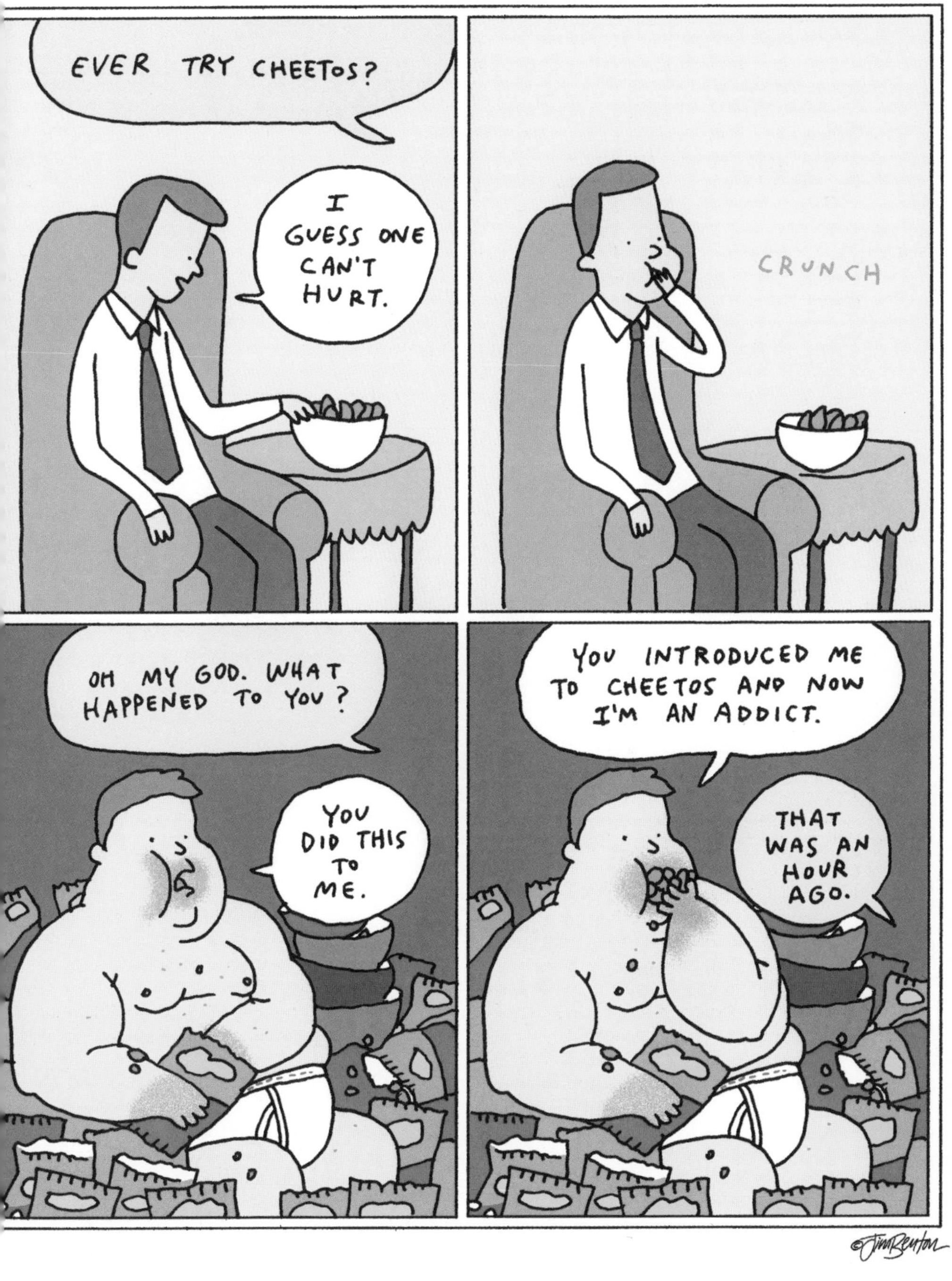
EVER TRY CHEETOS?
I GUESS ONE CAN'T HURT.
CRUNCH
OH MY GOD. WHAT HAPPENED TO YOU?
YOU DID THIS TO ME.
YOU INTRODUCED ME TO CHEETOS AND NOW I'M AN ADDICT.
THAT WAS AN HOUR AGO.
©JimBenton

A HELPFUL TIP

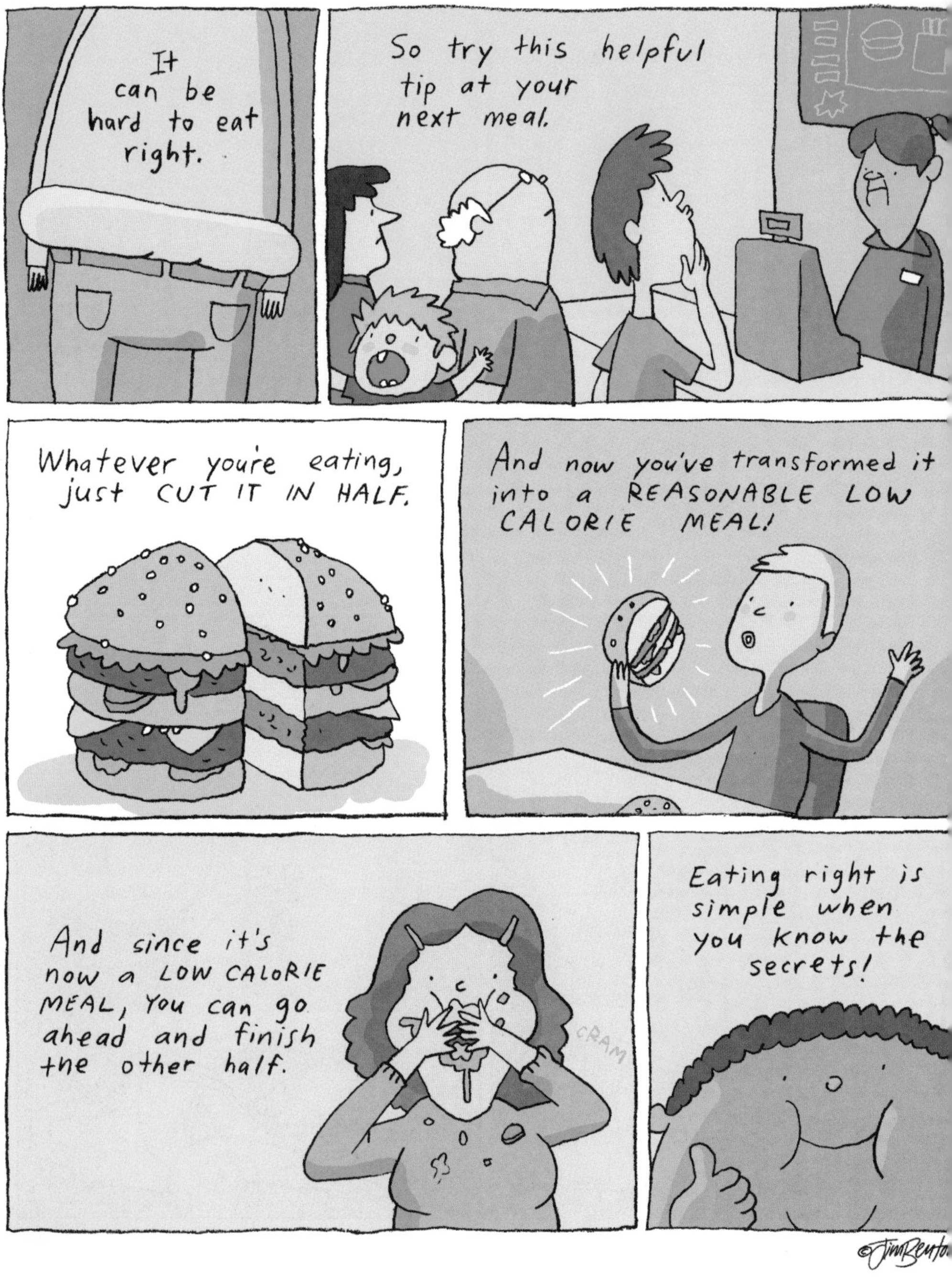
It can be hard to eat right.
So try this helpful tip at your next meal.
Whatever you're eating, just CUT IT IN HALF.
And now you've transformed it into a REASONABLE LOW CALORIE MEAL!
And since it's now a LOW CALORIE MEAL, you can go ahead and finish the other half.
CRAM
Eating right is simple when you know the secrets!

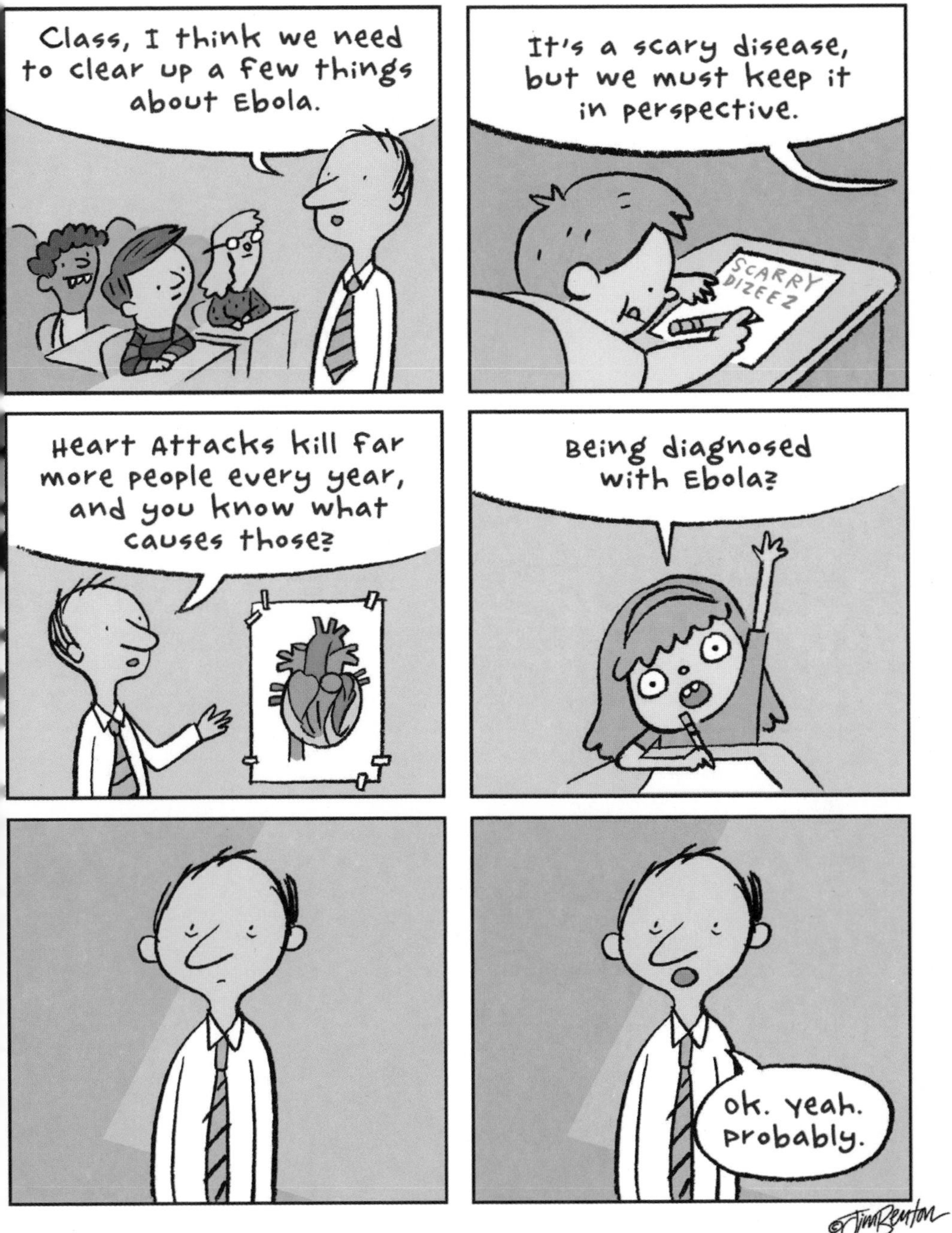
Class, I think we need to clear up a few things about Ebola.
It's a scary disease, but we must keep it in perspective.
SCARRY DIZEEZ
Heart Attacks kill far more people every year, and you know what causes those?
Being diagnosed with Ebola?
ok. yeah. probably.
©JimBenton

FART
HA!
One day I will NO LONGER FIND FARTS FUNNY.
FART
HA!
JUST KIDDING. UP YOURS.

©Jim Benton

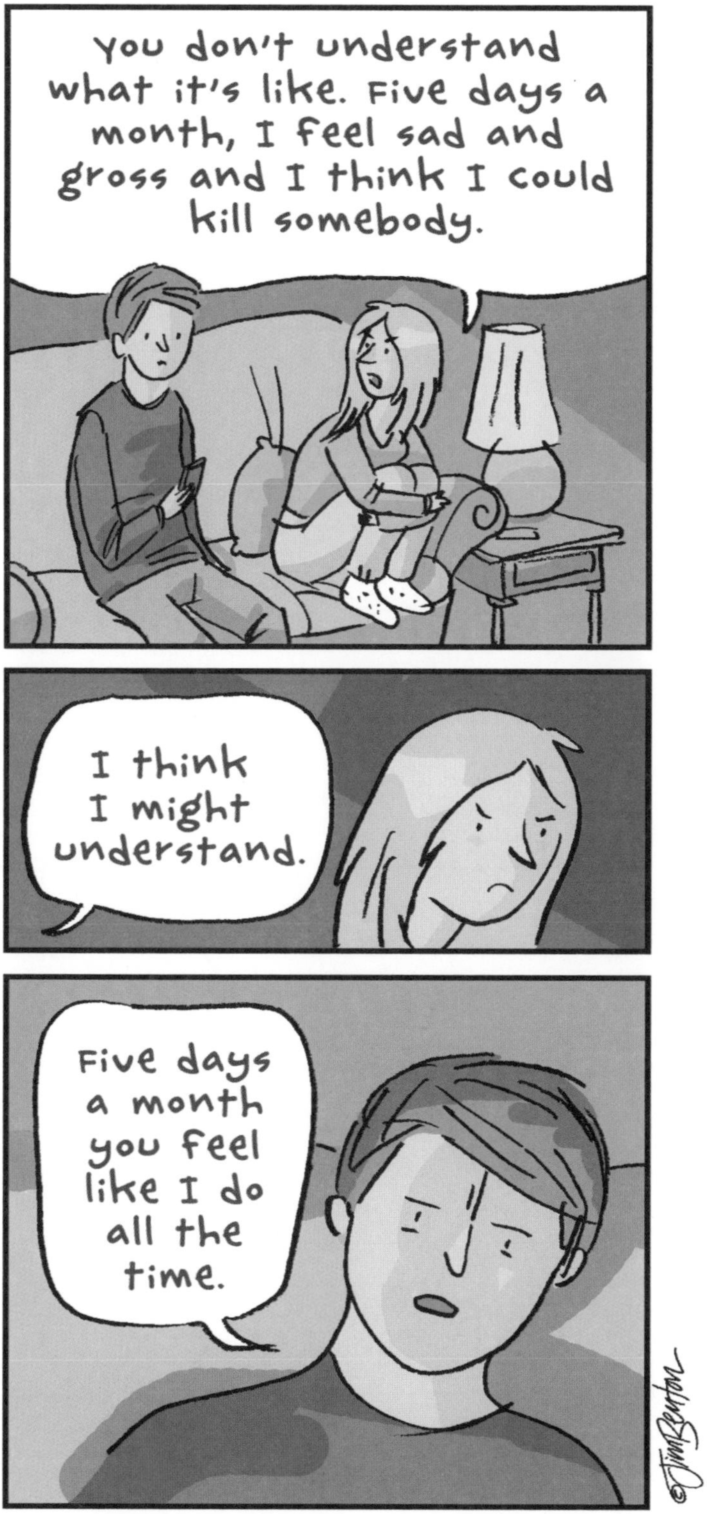
You don't understand what it's like. Five days a month, I feel sad and gross and I think I could kill somebody.
I think I might understand.
Five days a month you feel like I do all the time.

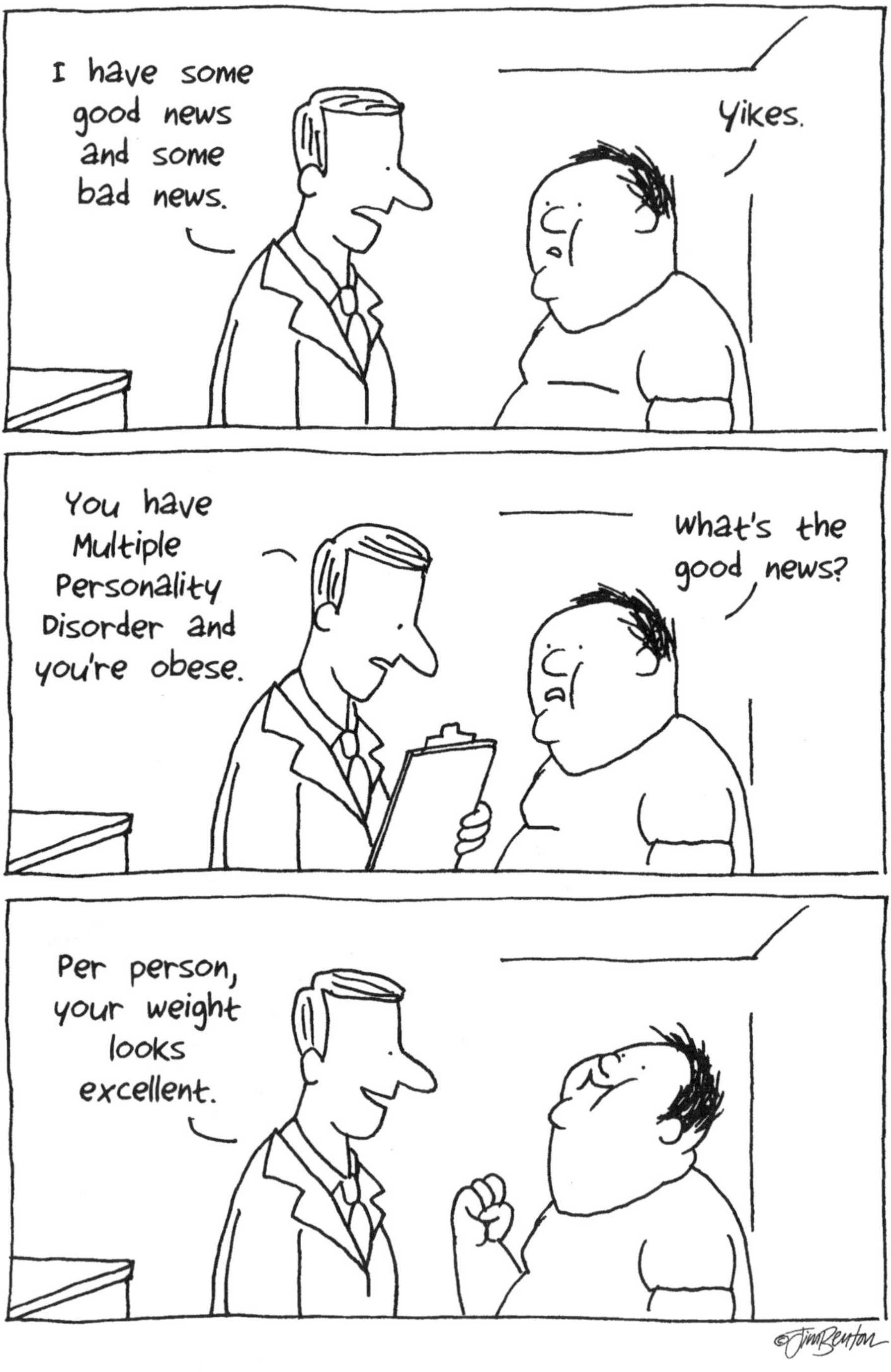
I have some good news and some bad news.
Yikes.
You have Multiple Personality Disorder and you're obese.
What's the good news?
Per person, your weight looks excellent.
©Jim Benton

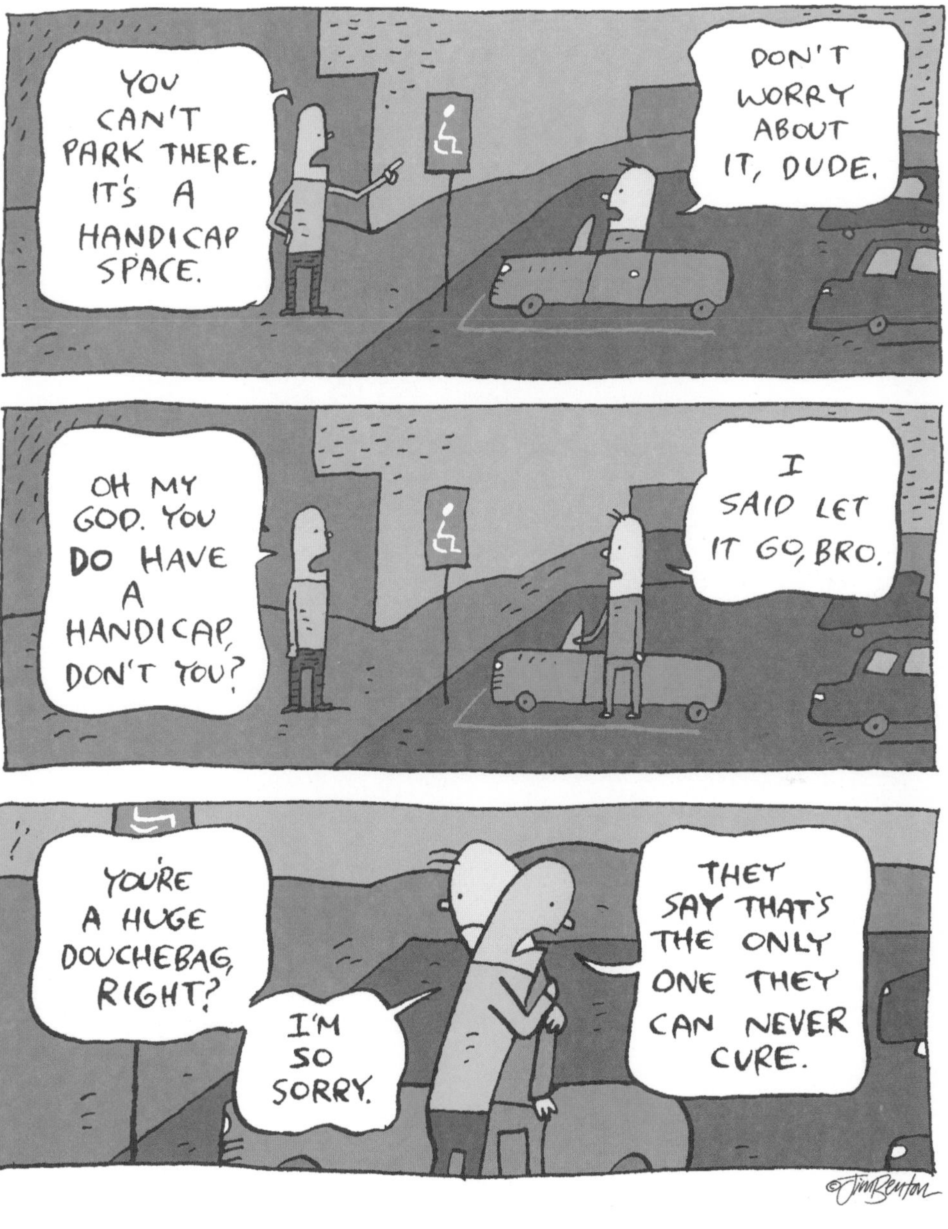
YOU CAN'T PARK THERE. IT'S A HANDICAP SPACE.
DON'T WORRY ABOUT IT, DUDE.
OH MY GOD. YOU DO HAVE A HANDICAP, DON'T YOU?
I SAID LET IT GO, BRO.
YOU'RE A HUGE DOUCHEBAG, RIGHT?
I'M SO SORRY.
THEY SAY THAT'S THE ONLY ONE THEY CAN NEVER CURE.
©Jim Benton

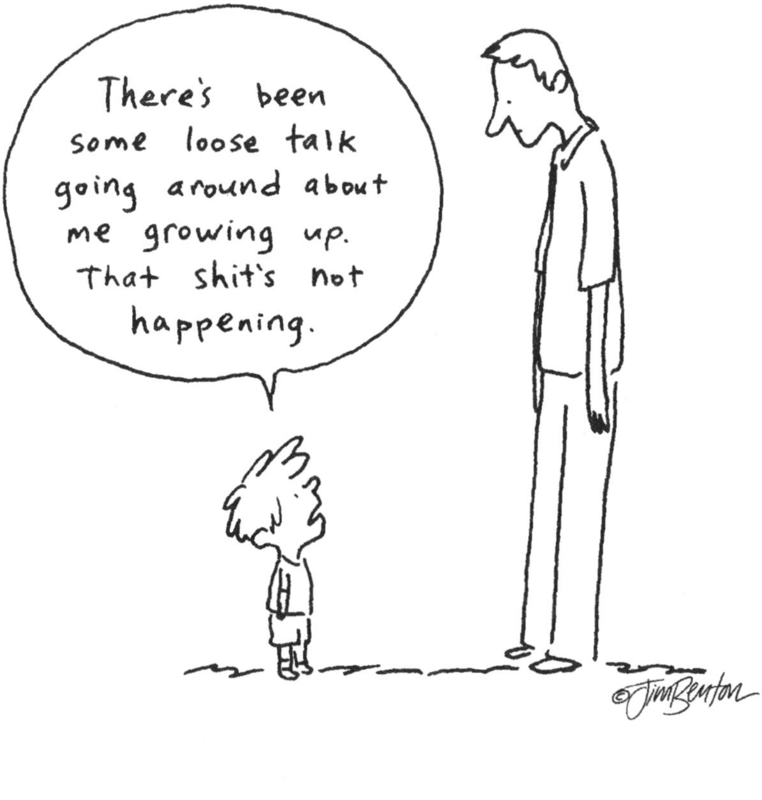
There's been some loose talk going around about me growing up. That shit's not happening.
©Jim Benton

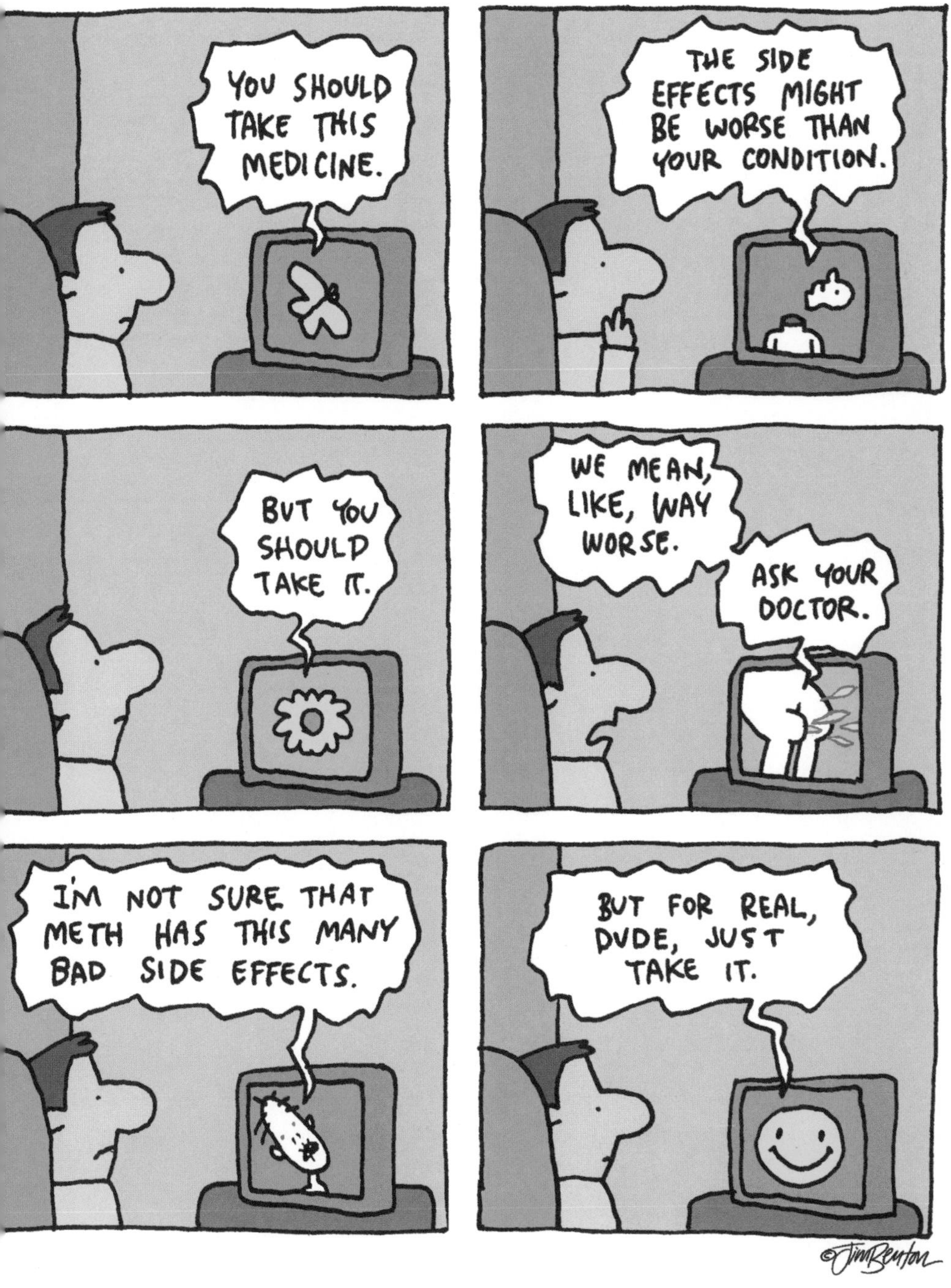
YOU SHOULD TAKE THIS MEDICINE.
THE SIDE EFFECTS MIGHT BE WORSE THAN YOUR CONDITION.
BUT YOU SHOULD TAKE IT.
WE MEAN, LIKE, WAY WORSE.
ASK YOUR DOCTOR.
I'M NOT SURE THAT METH HAS THIS MANY BAD SIDE EFFECTS.
BUT FOR REAL, DUDE, JUST TAKE IT.
©JimBenton

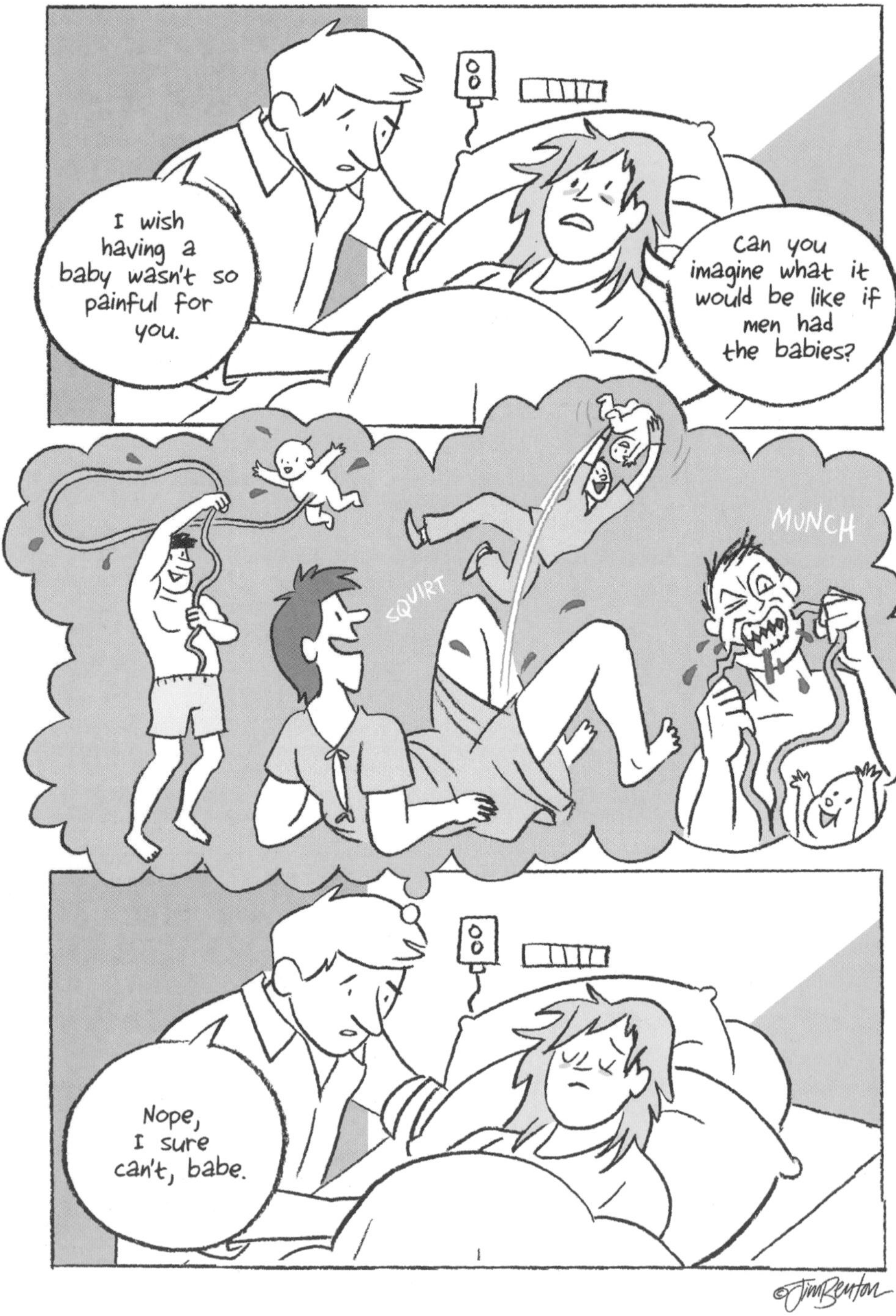
I wish having a baby wasn't so painful for you.
Can you imagine what it would be like if men had the babies?
SQUIRT
MUNCH
Nope, I sure can't, babe.
©Jim Benton

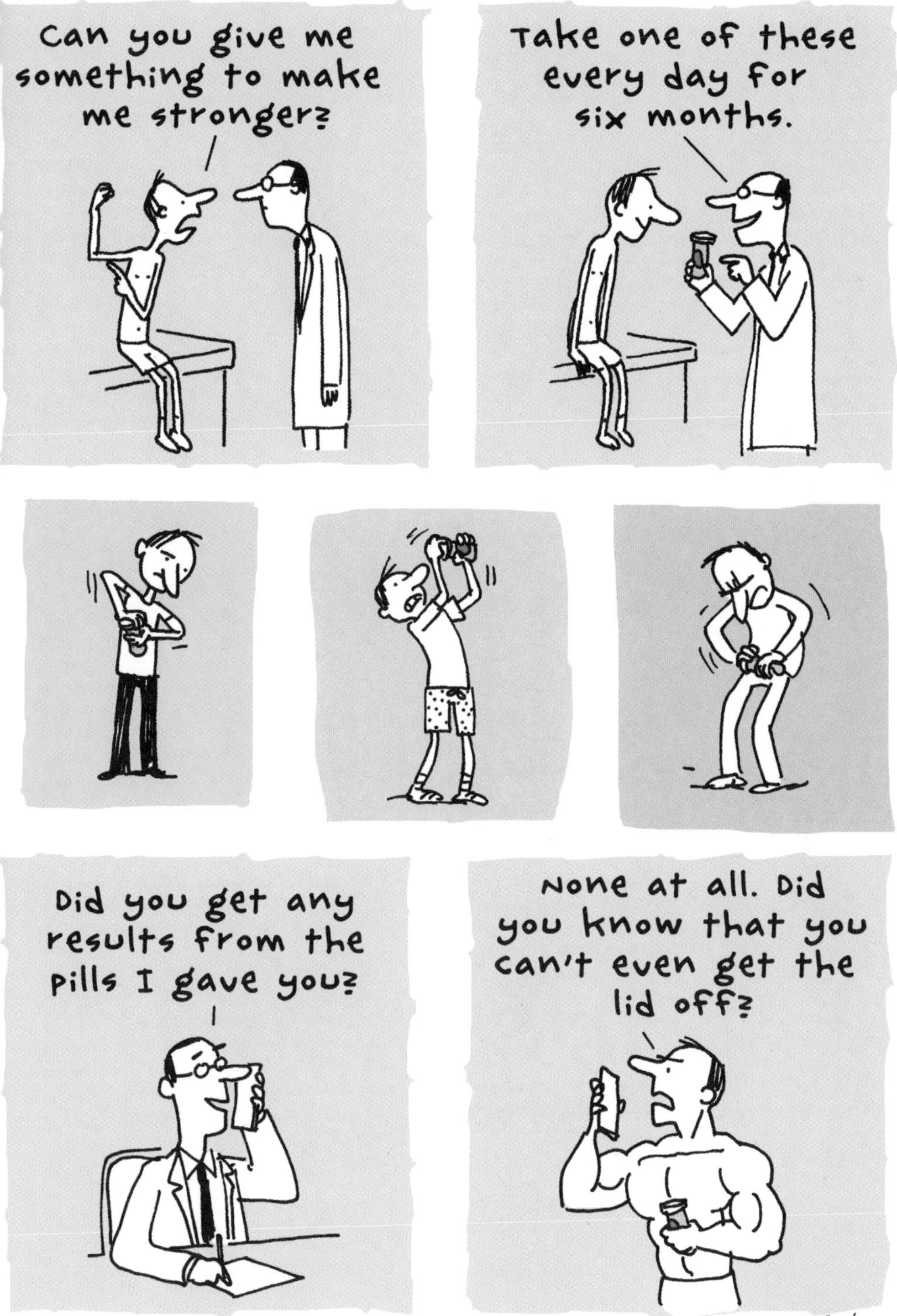
Can you give me something to make me stronger?
Take one of these every day for six months.
Did you get any results from the pills I gave you?
None at all. Did you know that you can't even get the lid off?
©Jim Benton

©Jim Benton

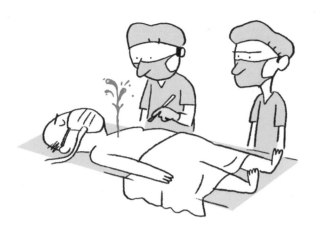

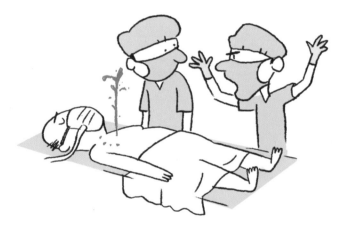

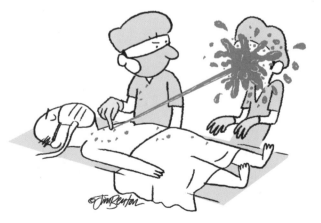

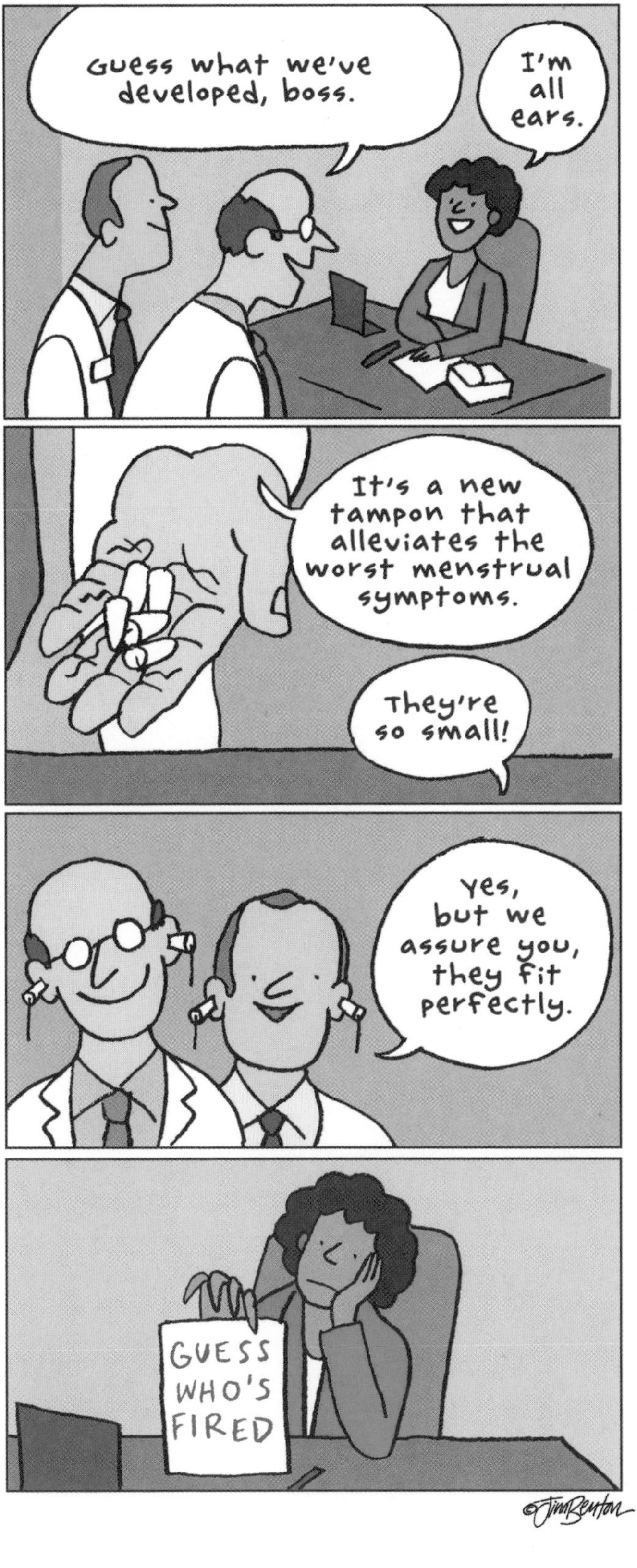
Guess what we've developed, boss.
I'm all ears.
It's a new tampon that alleviates the worst menstrual symptoms.
They're so small!
Yes, but we assure you, they fit perfectly.
GUESS WHO'S FIRED
©Jim Benton

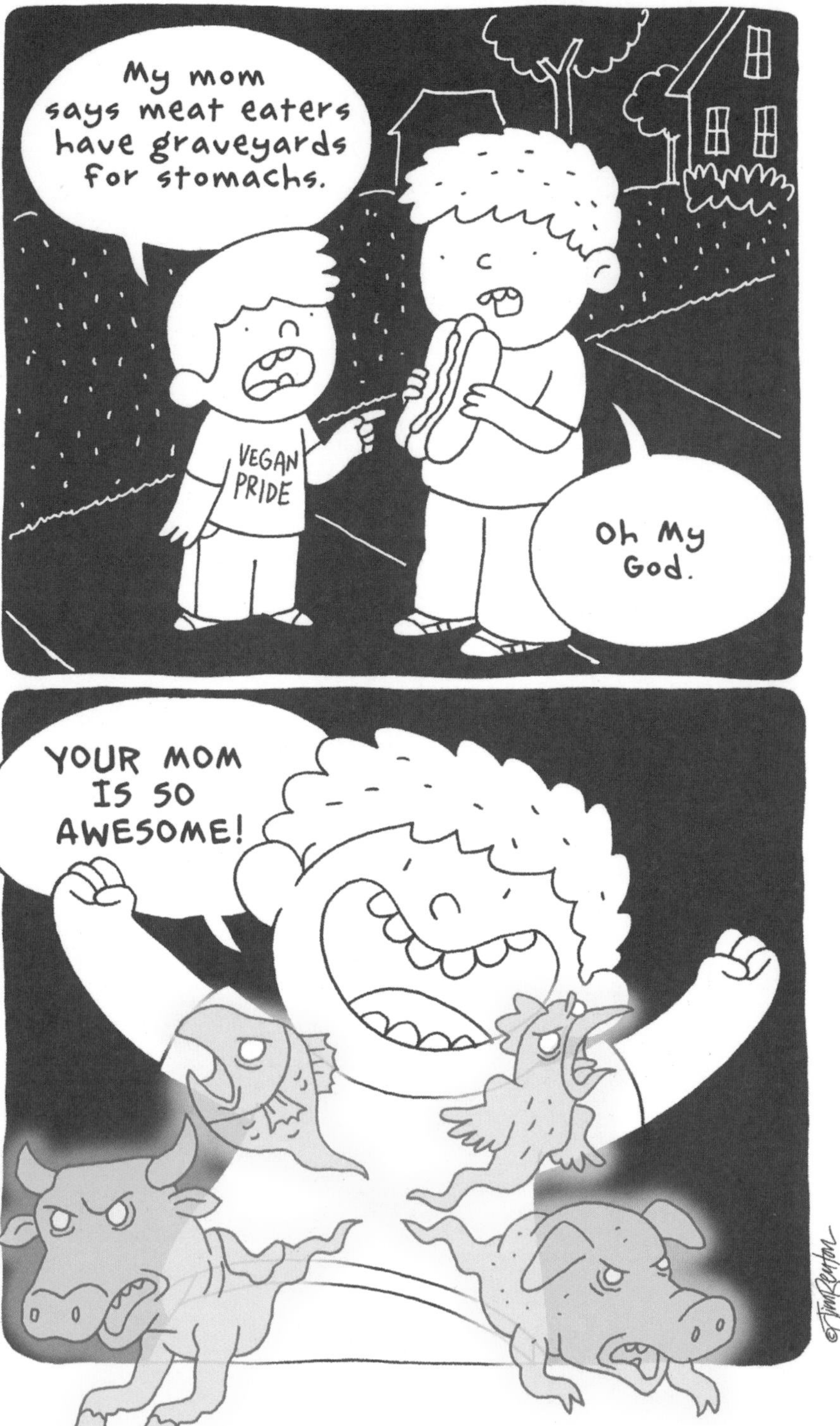
My mom says meat eaters have graveyards for stomachs.
VEGAN PRIDE
Oh My God.
YOUR MOM IS SO AWESOME!

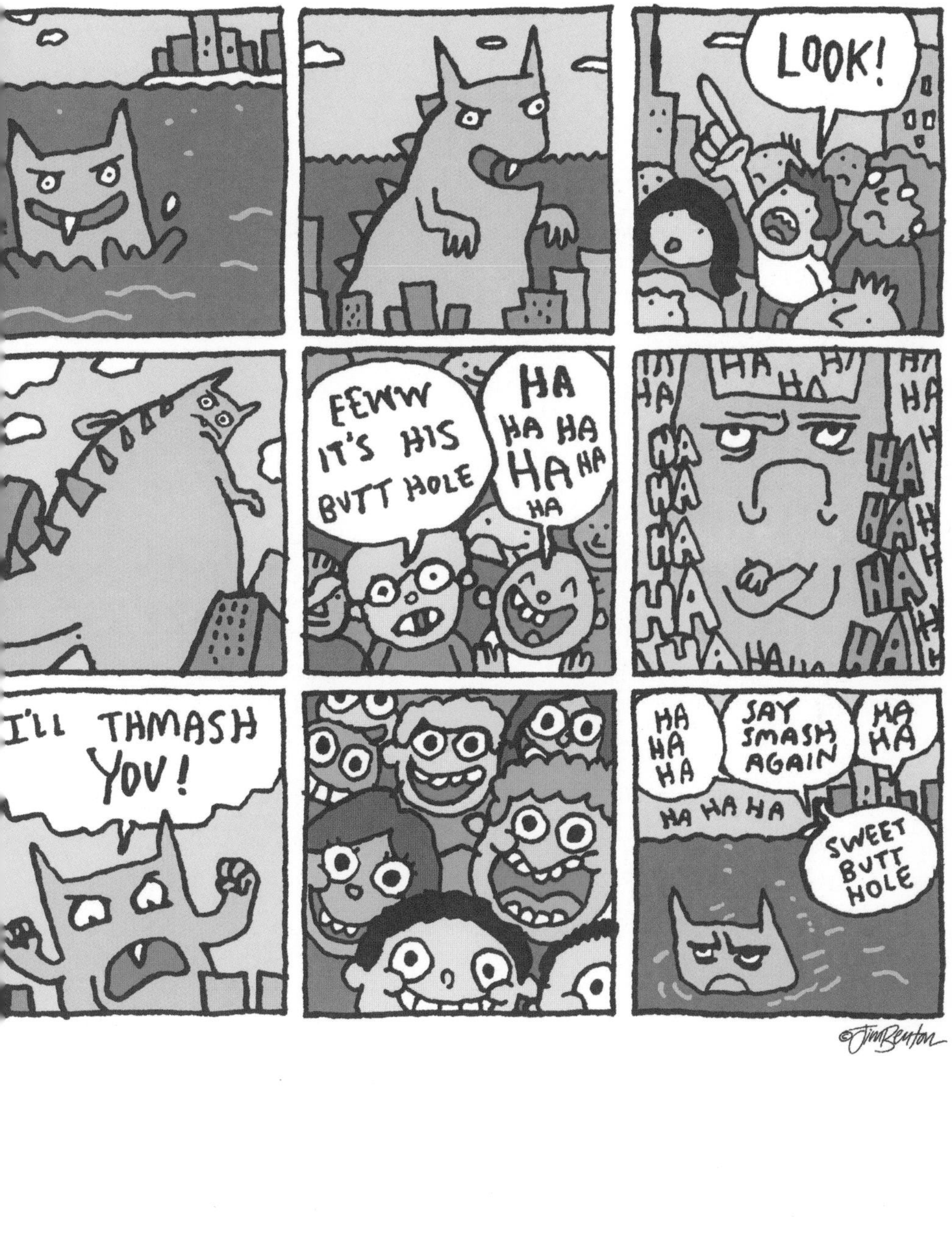
LOOK!
EEWW IT'S HIS BUTT HOLE
HA HA HA HA HA HA
I'LL THMASH YOU!
HA HA HA
SAY SMASH AGAIN
HA HA
HA HA HA
SWEET BUTT HOLE
©Jim Benton

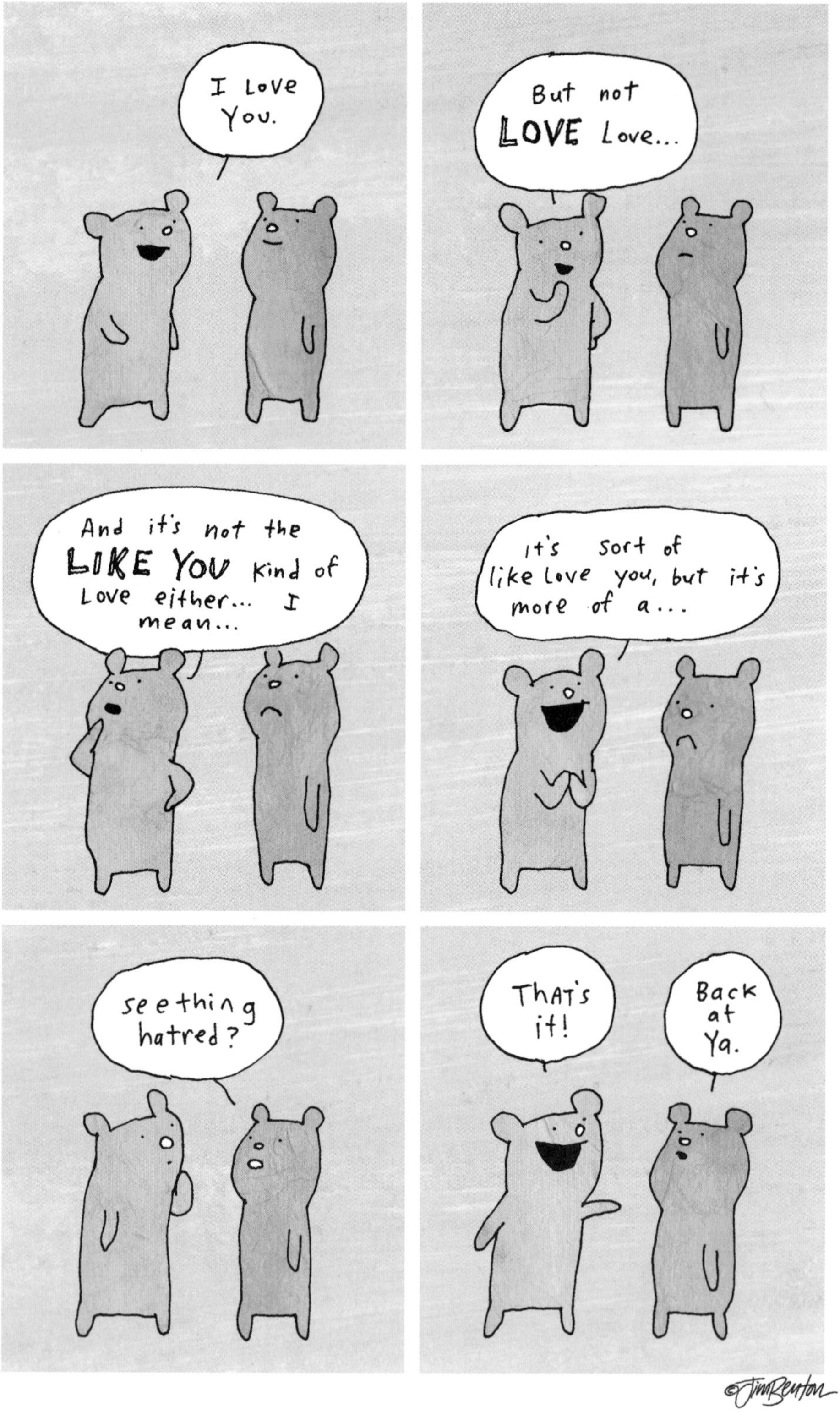
I love you.
But not LOVE love...
And it's not the LIKE YOU kind of love either... I mean...
It's sort of like love you, but it's more of a...
seething hatred?
THAT'S it!
Back at ya.
©Jim Benton

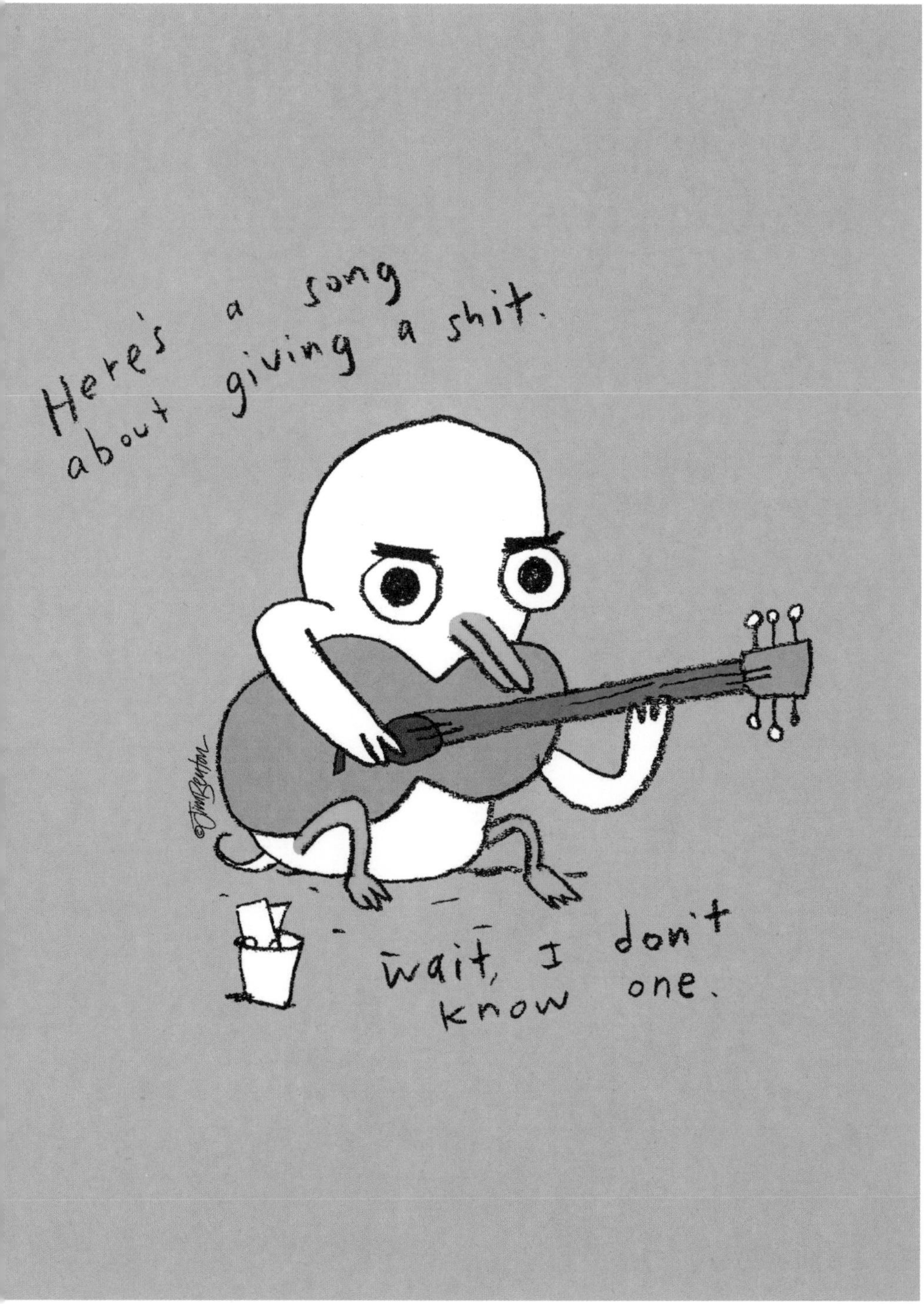

Here's a song about giving a shit.
wait, I don't know one.
©Jim Benton

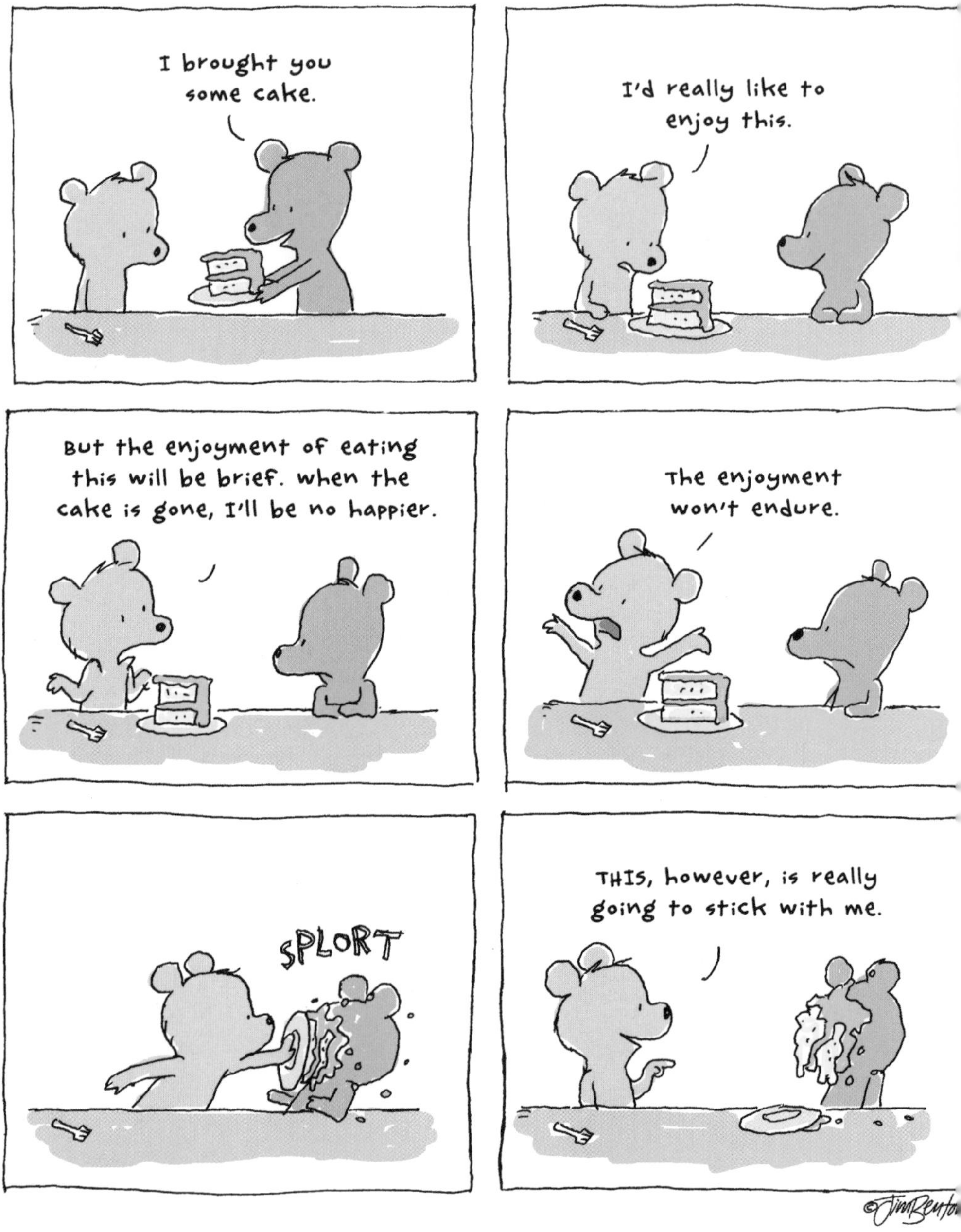
I brought you some cake.
I'd really like to enjoy this.
But the enjoyment of eating this will be brief. When the cake is gone, I'll be no happier.
The enjoyment won't endure.
SPLORT
THIS, however, is really going to stick with me.
©Jim Benton

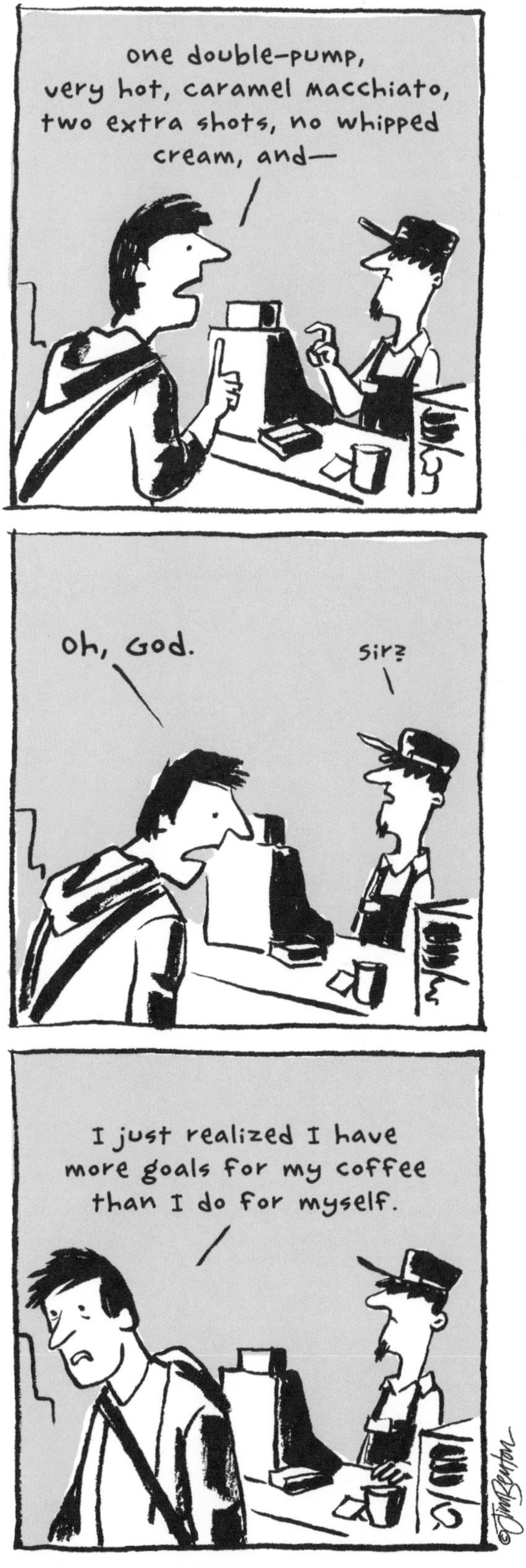
one double-pump, very hot, caramel macchiato, two extra shots, no whipped cream, and—
Oh, God.
Sir?
I just realized I have more goals for my coffee than I do for myself.

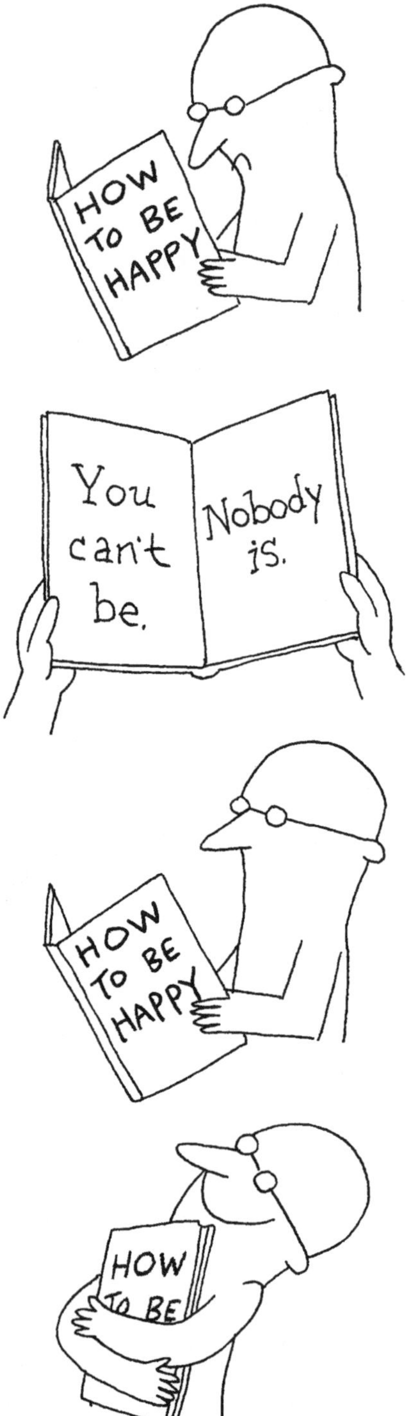
HOW TO BE HAPPY
You can't be.
Nobody is.
HOW TO BE HAPPY
HOW TO BE
©Jim Benton

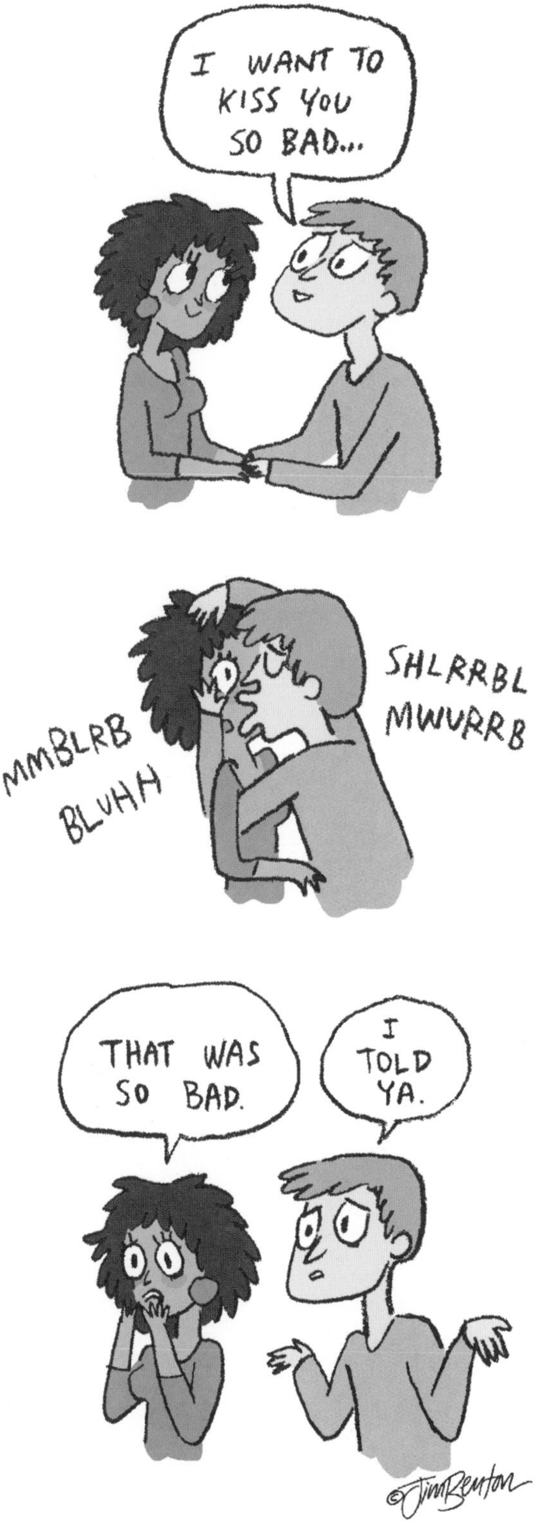
I WANT TO KISS YOU SO BAD...
SHLRRBL MWURRB
MMBLRB BLUHH
THAT WAS SO BAD.
I TOLD YA.
©Jim Benton

I'm really super sorry.

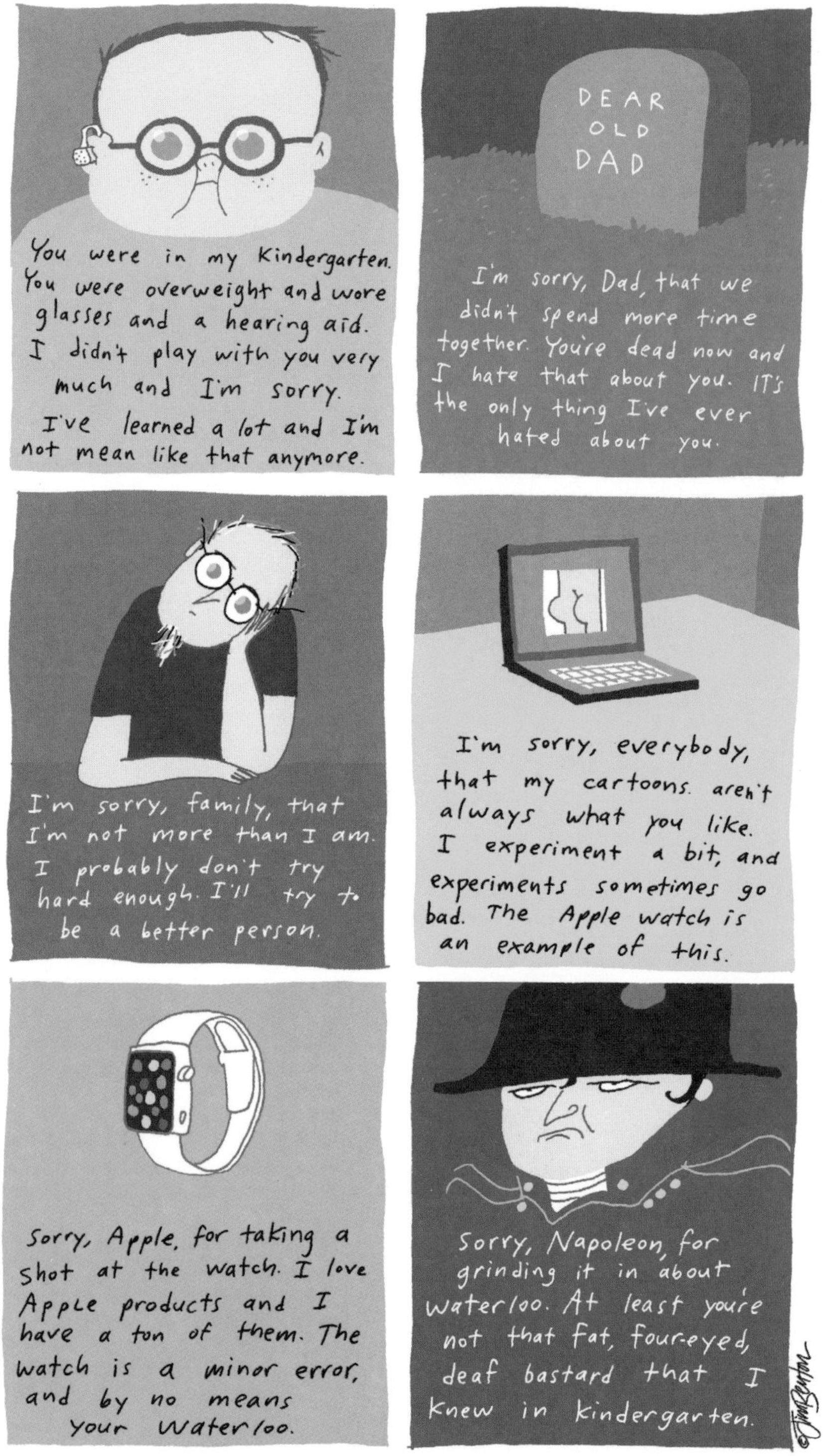
You were in my Kindergarten. You were overweight and wore glasses and a hearing aid. I didn't play with you very much and I'm sorry. I've learned a lot and I'm not mean like that anymore.
DEAR OLD DAD
I'm sorry, Dad, that we didn't spend more time together. You're dead now and I hate that about you. IT's the only thing I've ever hated about you.
I'm sorry, family, that I'm not more than I am. I probably don't try hard enough. I'll try to be a better person.
I'm sorry, everybody, that my cartoons aren't always what you like. I experiment a bit, and experiments sometimes go bad. The Apple watch is an example of this.
Sorry, Apple, for taking a shot at the watch. I love Apple products and I have a ton of them. The watch is a minor error, and by no means your Waterloo.
Sorry, Napoleon, for grinding it in about Waterloo. At least you're not that fat, four-eyed, deaf bastard that I knew in kindergarten.

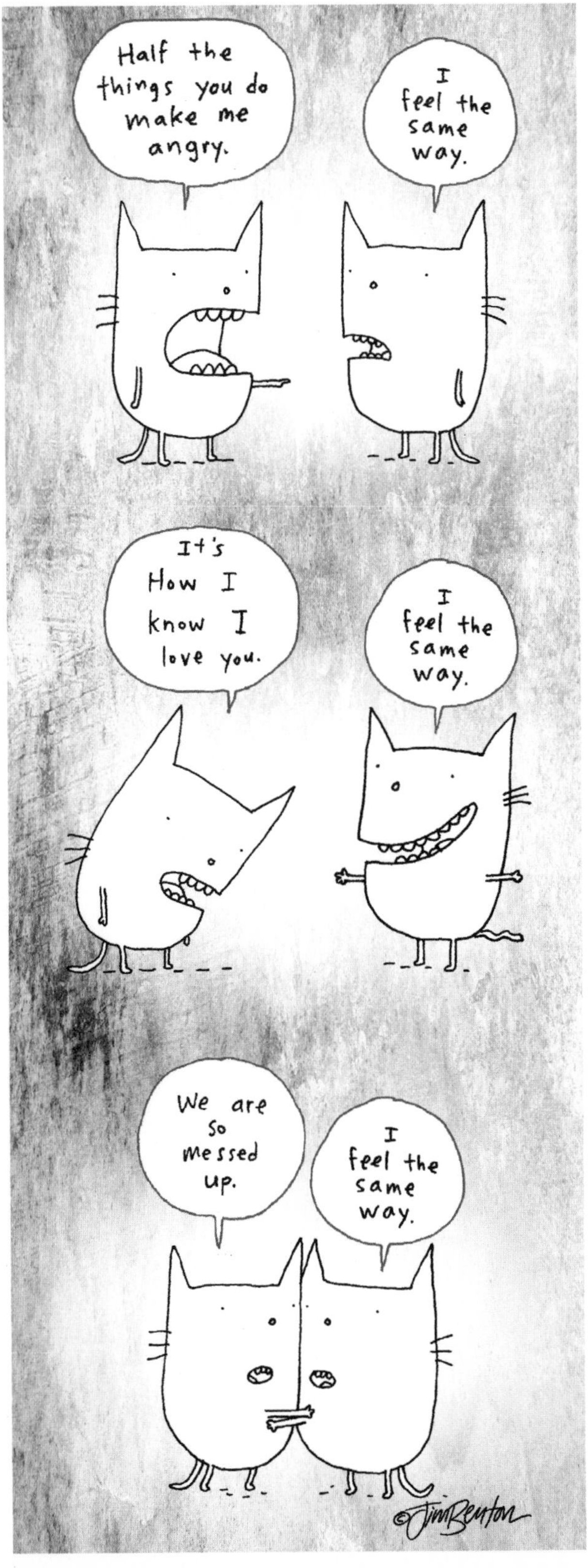
Half the things you do make me angry.
I feel the same way.
It's How I know I love you.
I feel the same way.
We are so messed up.
I feel the same way.
©Jim Benton

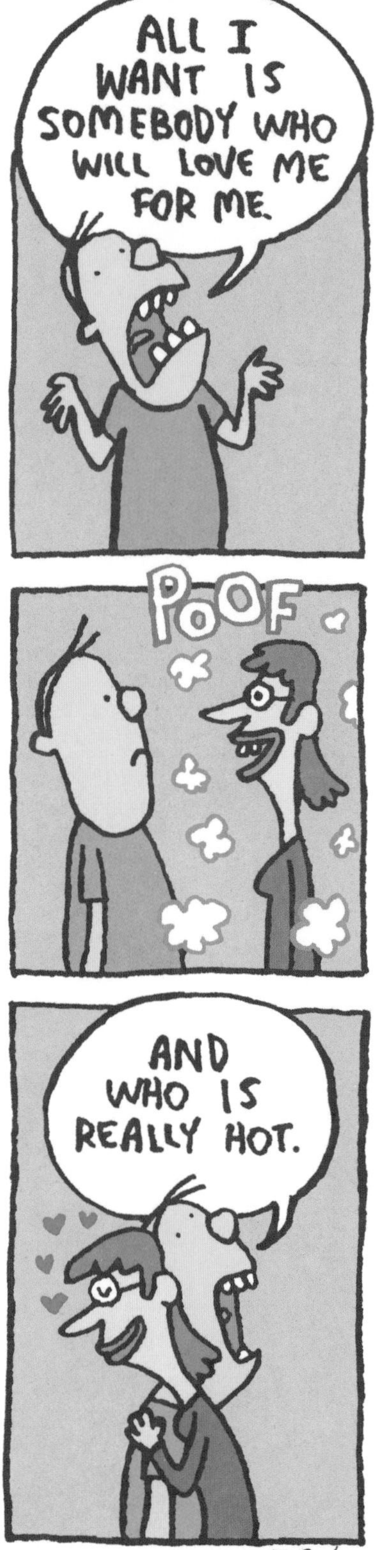
ALL I WANT IS SOMEBODY WHO WILL LOVE ME FOR ME.
POOF
AND WHO IS REALLY HOT.
©Jim Benton

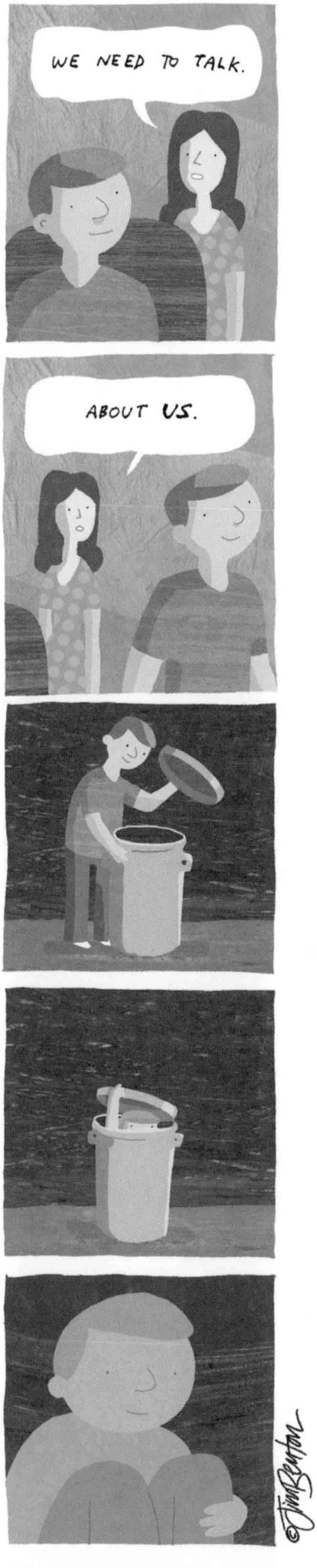
WE NEED TO TALK.
ABOUT US.

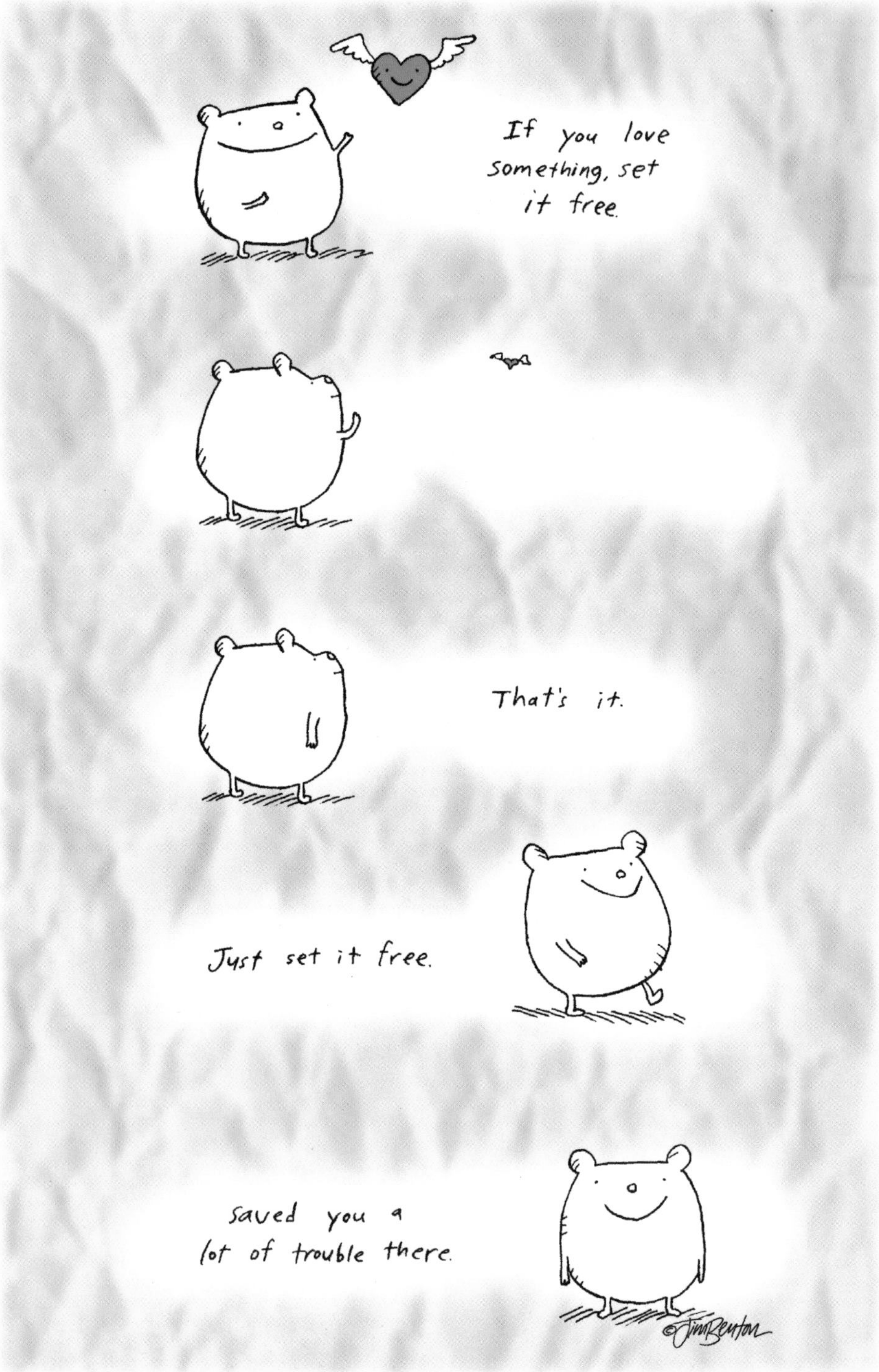
If you love something, set it free.
That's it.
Just set it free.
Saved you a lot of trouble there.
©Jim Benton

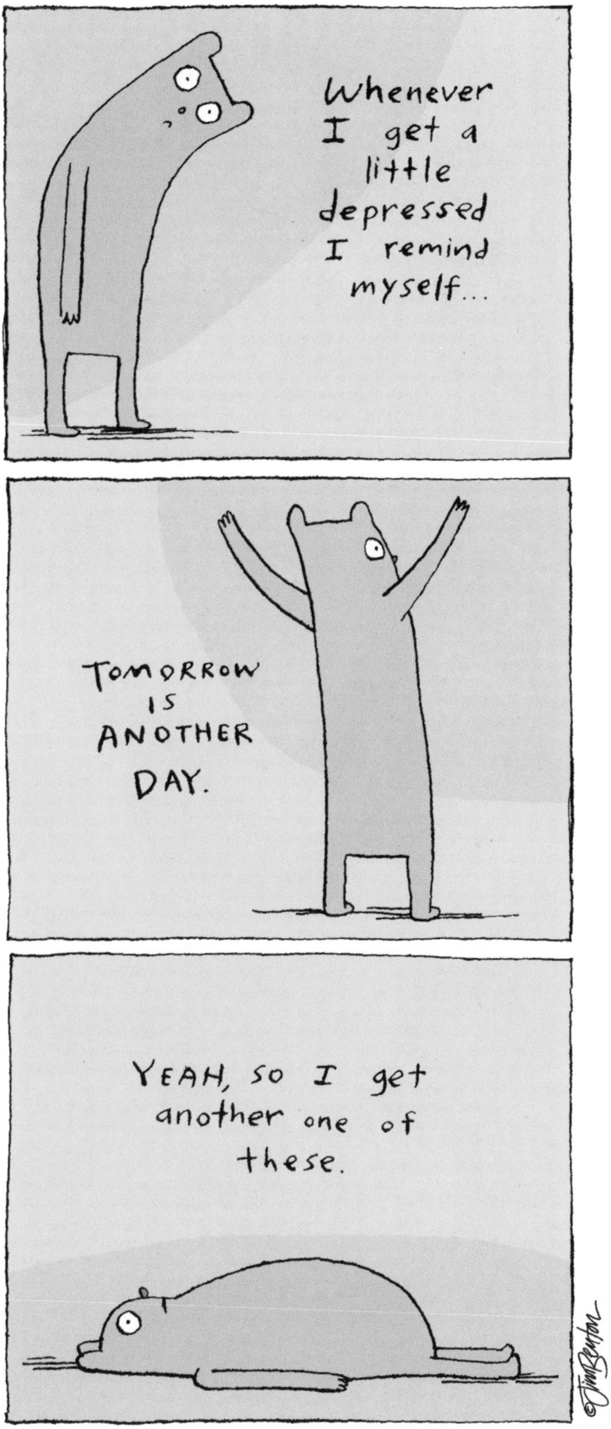
Whenever I get a little depressed I remind myself...
TOMORROW IS ANOTHER DAY.
YEAH, SO I get another one of these.

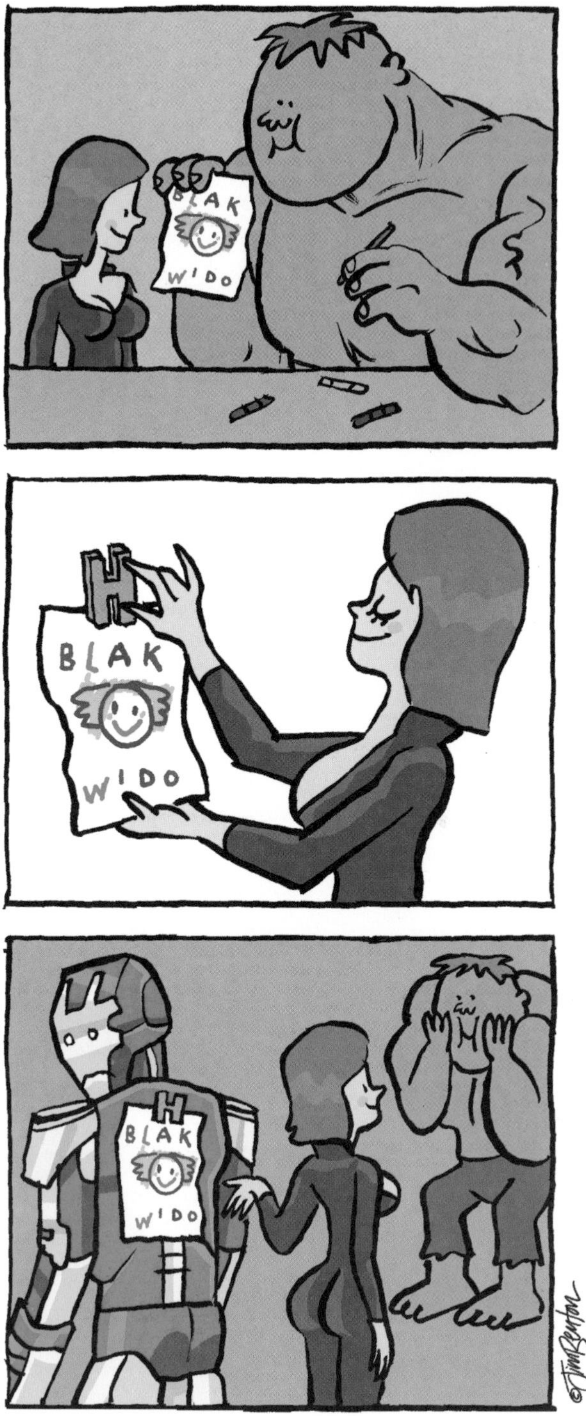
BLAK
WIDO
H
BLAK
WIDO
H
BLAK
WIDO
©Jim Benton

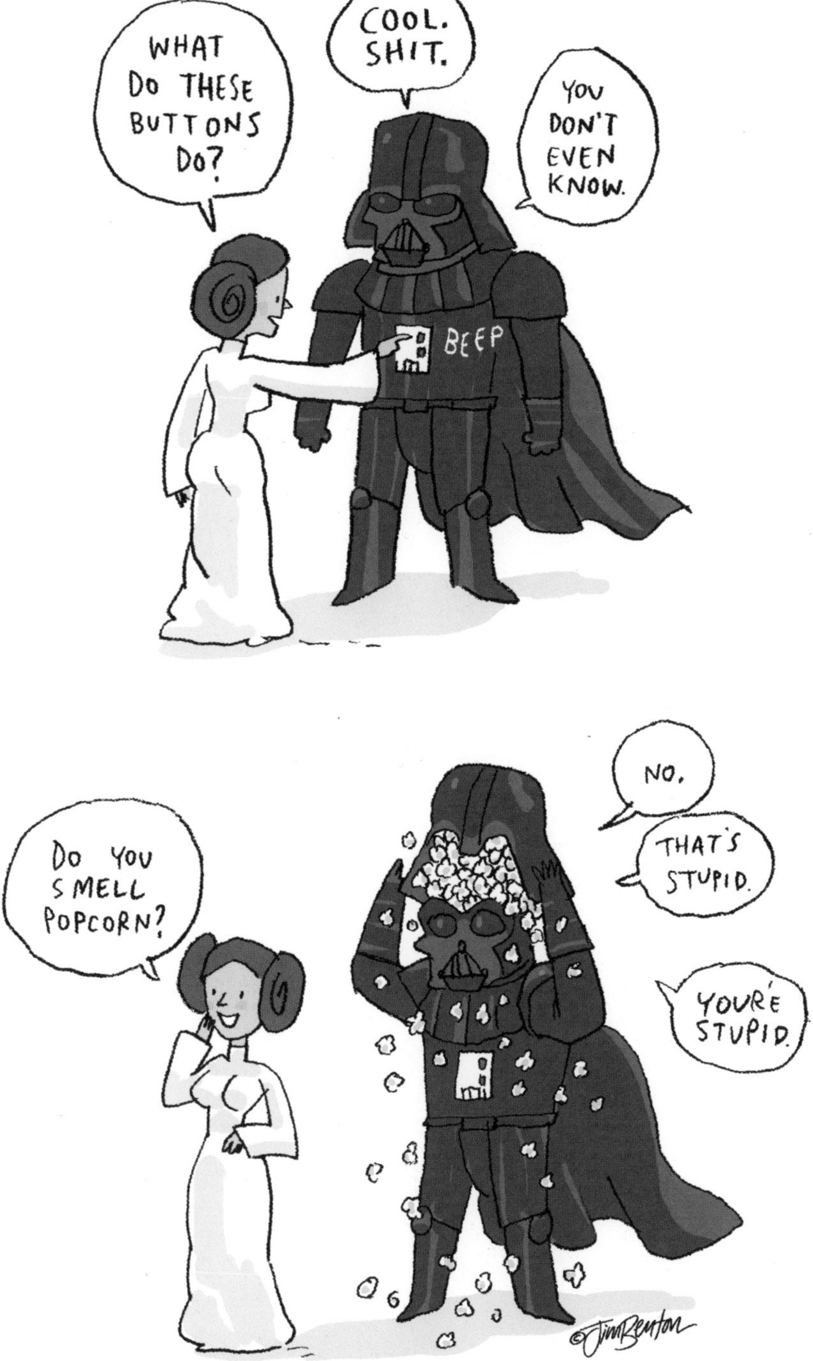
WHAT DO THESE BUTTONS DO?
COOL. SHIT.
YOU DON'T EVEN KNOW.
BEEP
DO YOU SMELL POPCORN?
NO.
THAT'S STUPID.
YOU'RE STUPID.
©Jim Benton

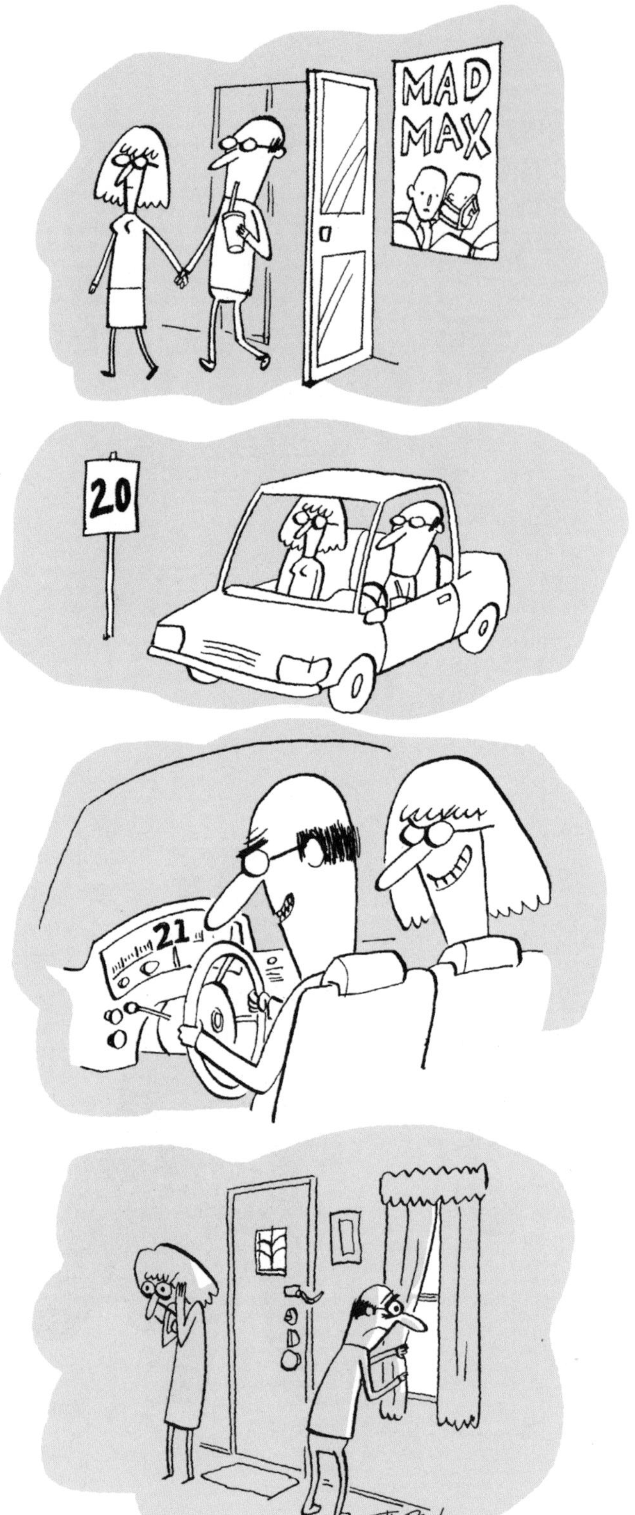
MAD MAX
20
21
©Jim Benton

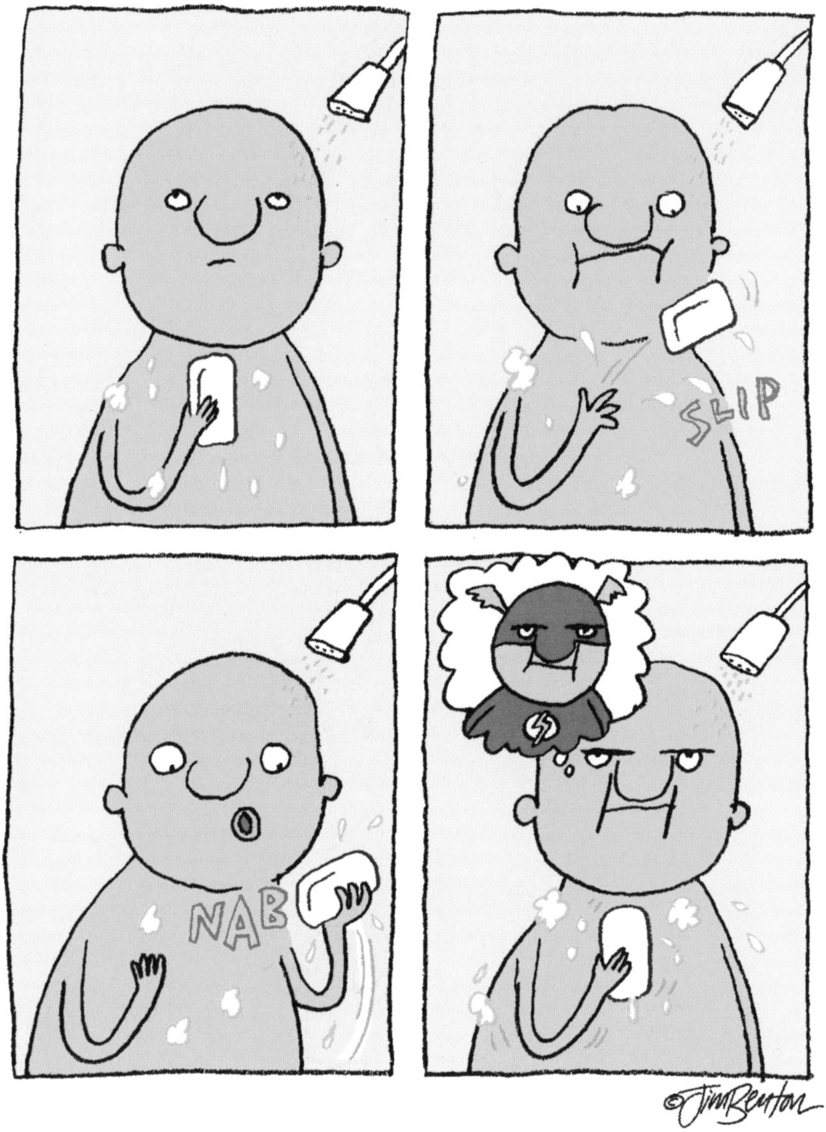
SLIP
NAB
©Jim Benton

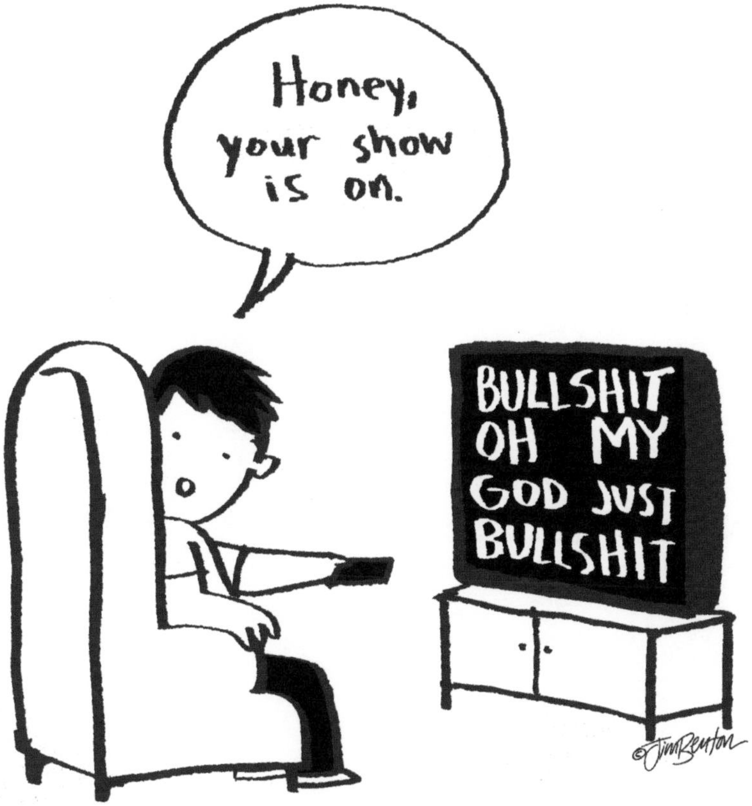
Honey, your show is on.
BULLSHIT OH MY GOD JUST BULLSHIT
©JimBenton

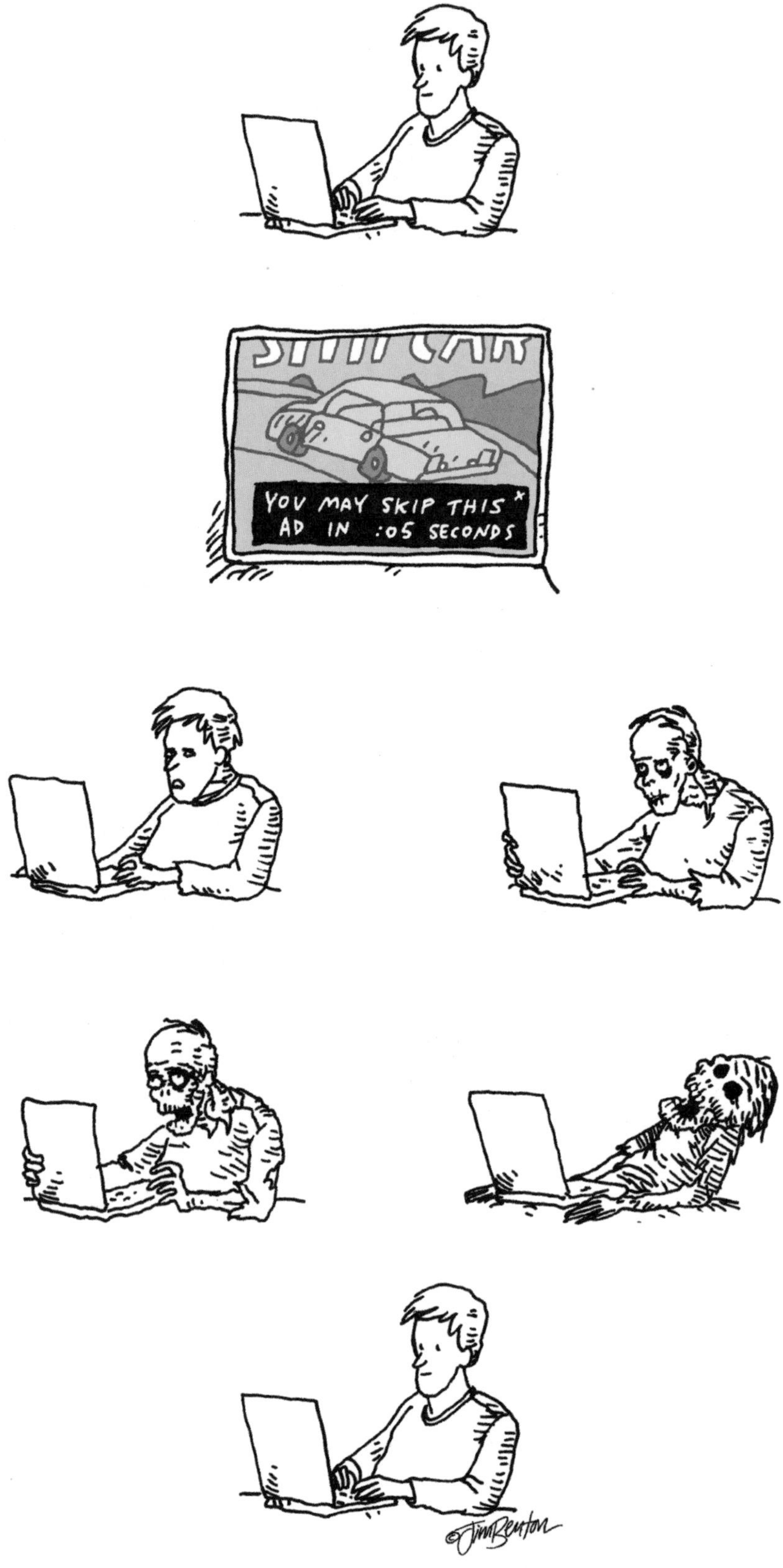
YOU MAY SKIP THIS* AD IN :05 SECONDS
©Jim Benton

©Jim Benton

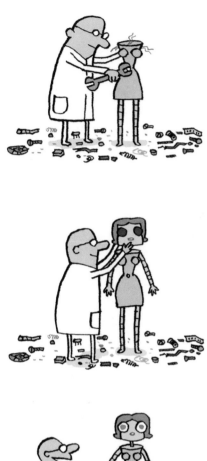

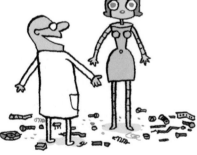

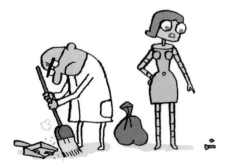

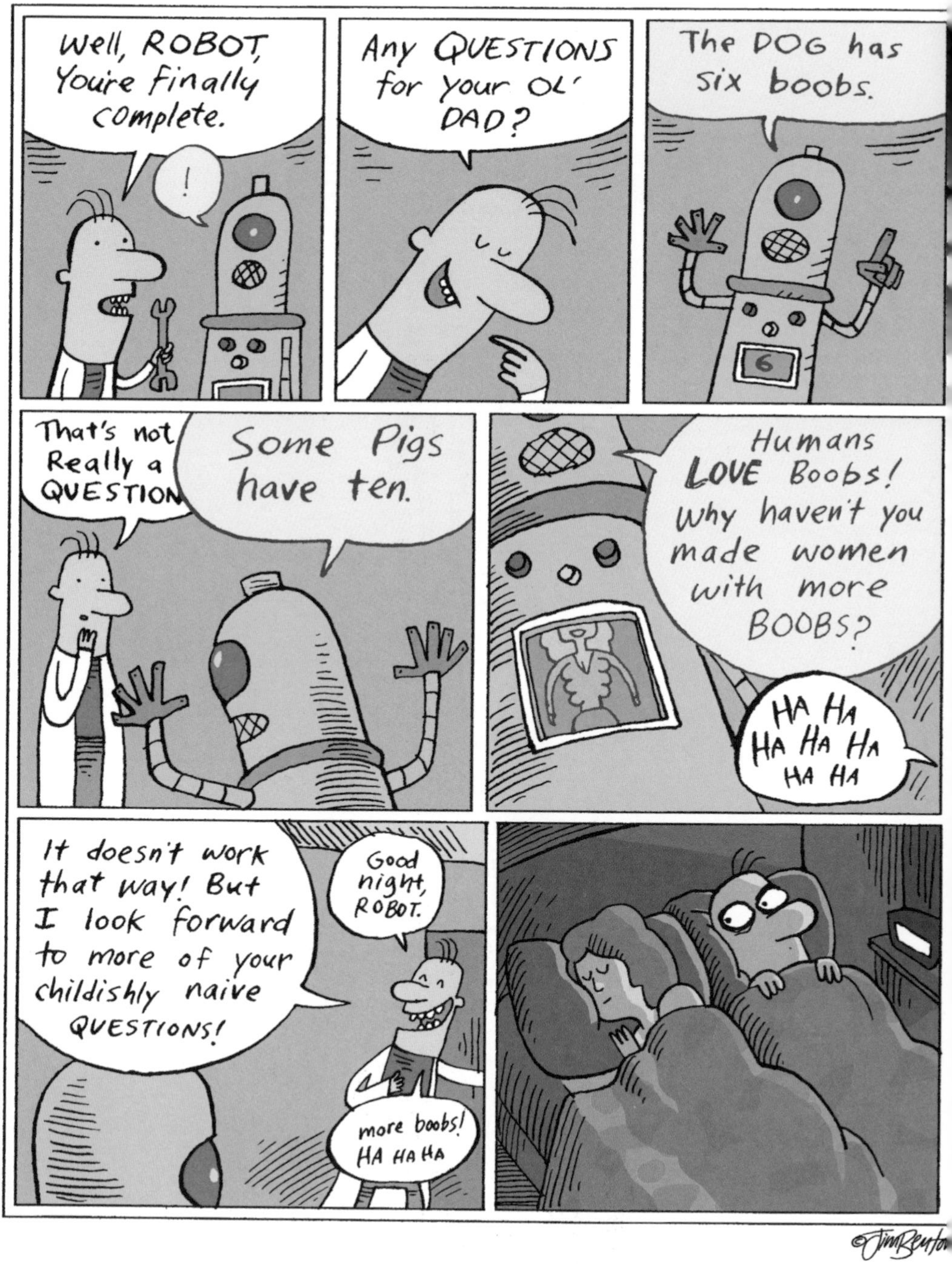

Well, ROBOT, You're Finally complete.
!
Any QUESTIONS for your OL' DAD?
The DOG has six boobs.
6
That's not Really a QUESTION
Some Pigs have ten.
Humans LOVE Boobs! Why haven't you made women with more BOOBS?
HA HA HA HA HA HA HA
It doesn't work that way! But I look forward to more of your childishly naive QUESTIONS!
Good night, ROBOT.
more boobs! HA HA HA
©JimBenton

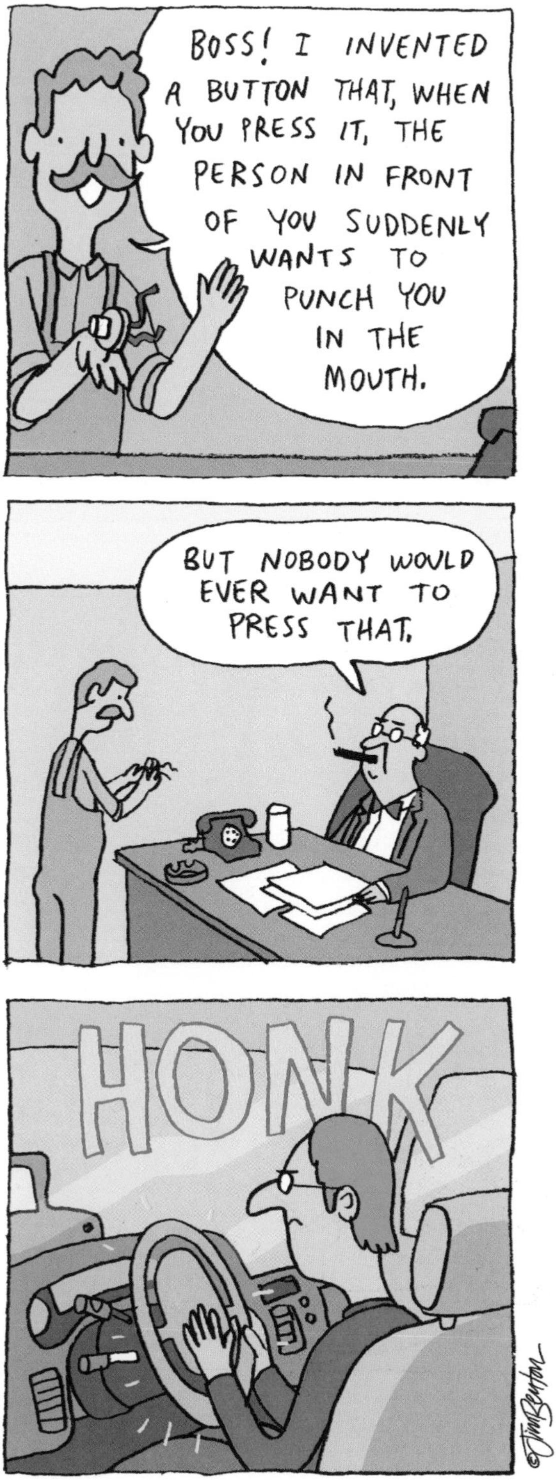
BOSS! I INVENTED A BUTTON THAT, WHEN YOU PRESS IT, THE PERSON IN FRONT OF YOU SUDDENLY WANTS TO PUNCH YOU IN THE MOUTH.
BUT NOBODY WOULD EVER WANT TO PRESS THAT.
HONK
©Jim Benton

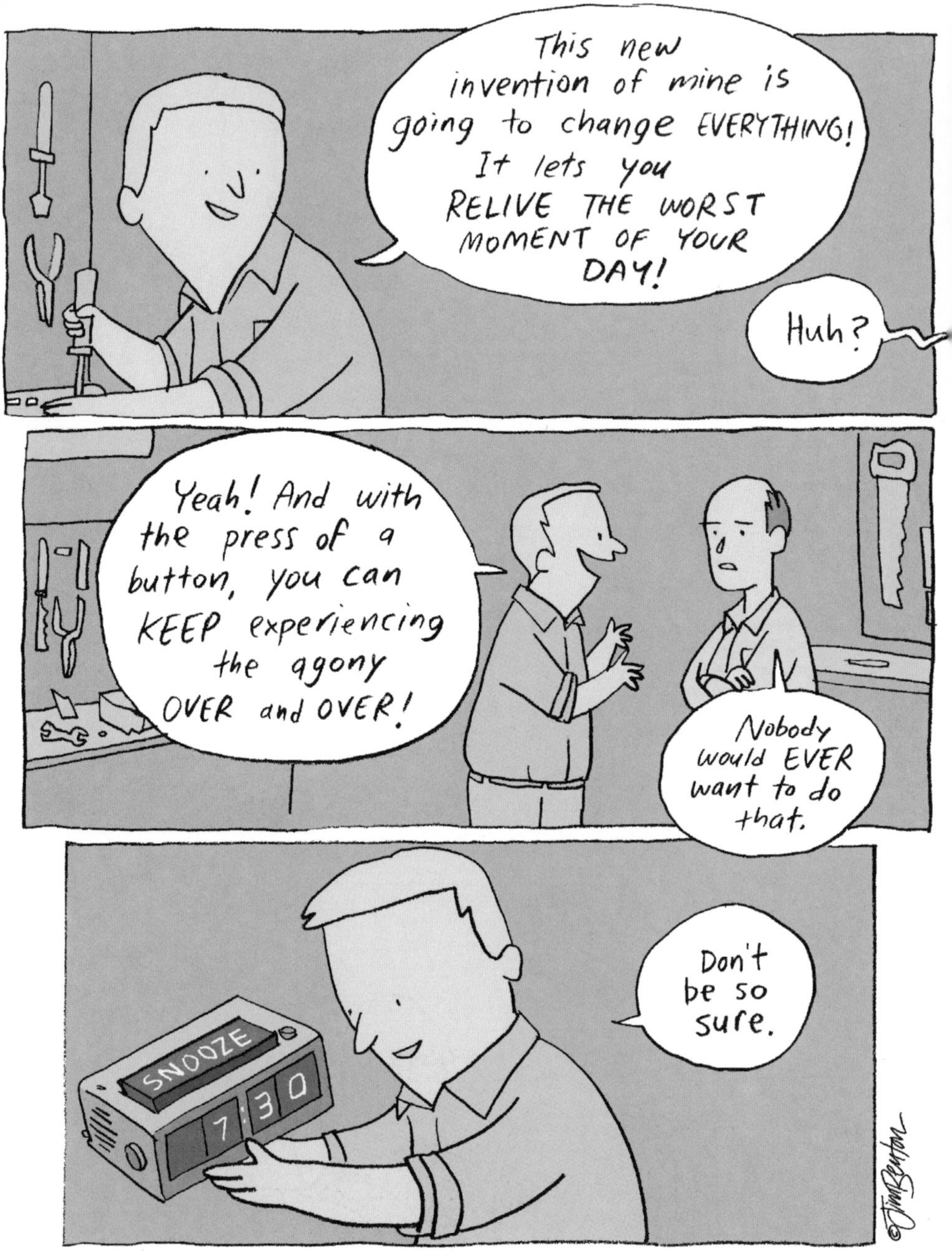

This new invention of mine is going to change EVERYTHING! It lets you RELIVE THE WORST MOMENT OF YOUR DAY!
Huh?
Yeah! And with the press of a button, you can KEEP experiencing the agony OVER and OVER!
Nobody would EVER want to do that.
SNOOZE
7:30
Don't be so sure.
©Jim Benton

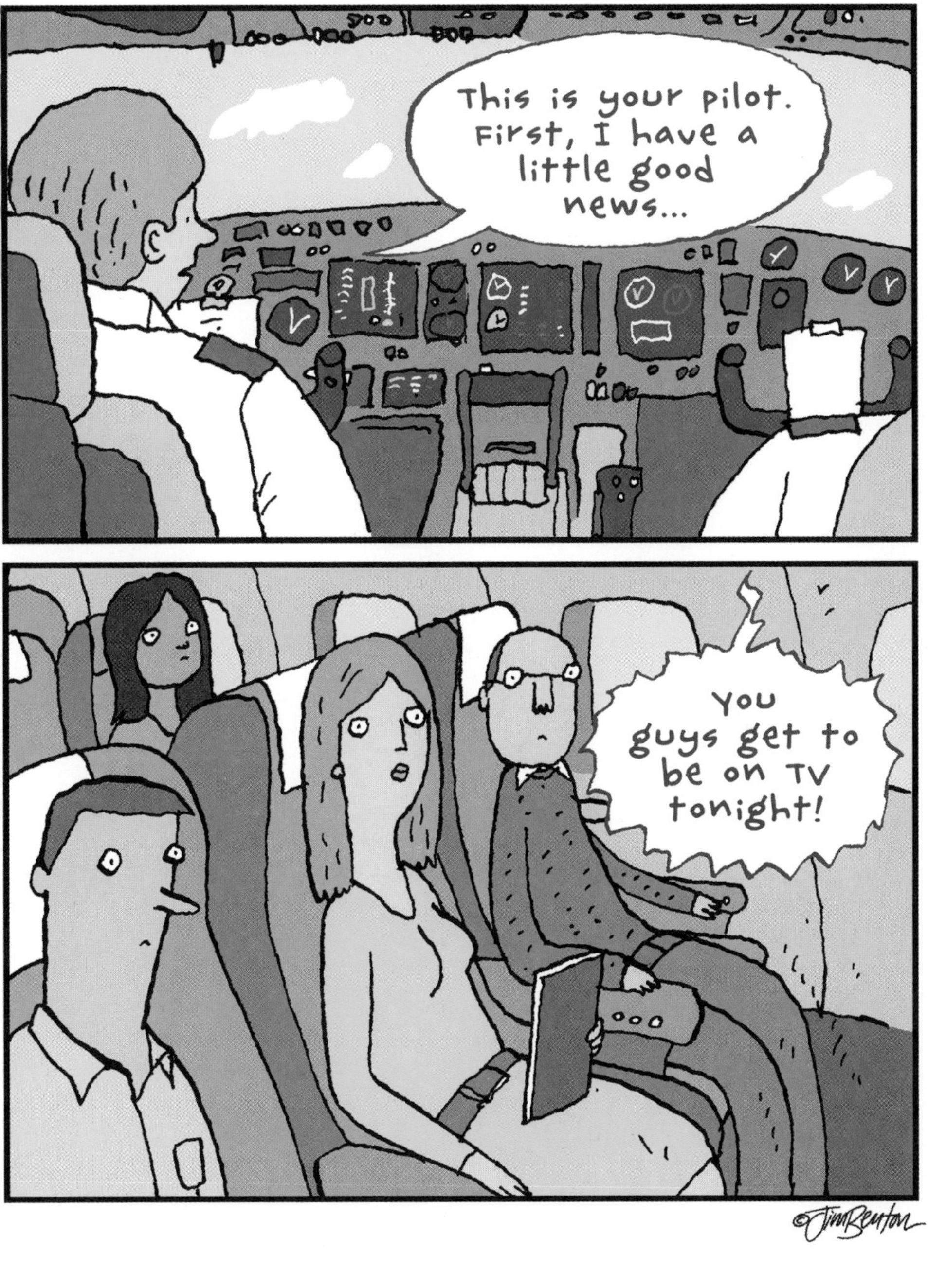
This is your pilot. First, I have a little good news...
You guys get to be on TV tonight!
©Jim Benton

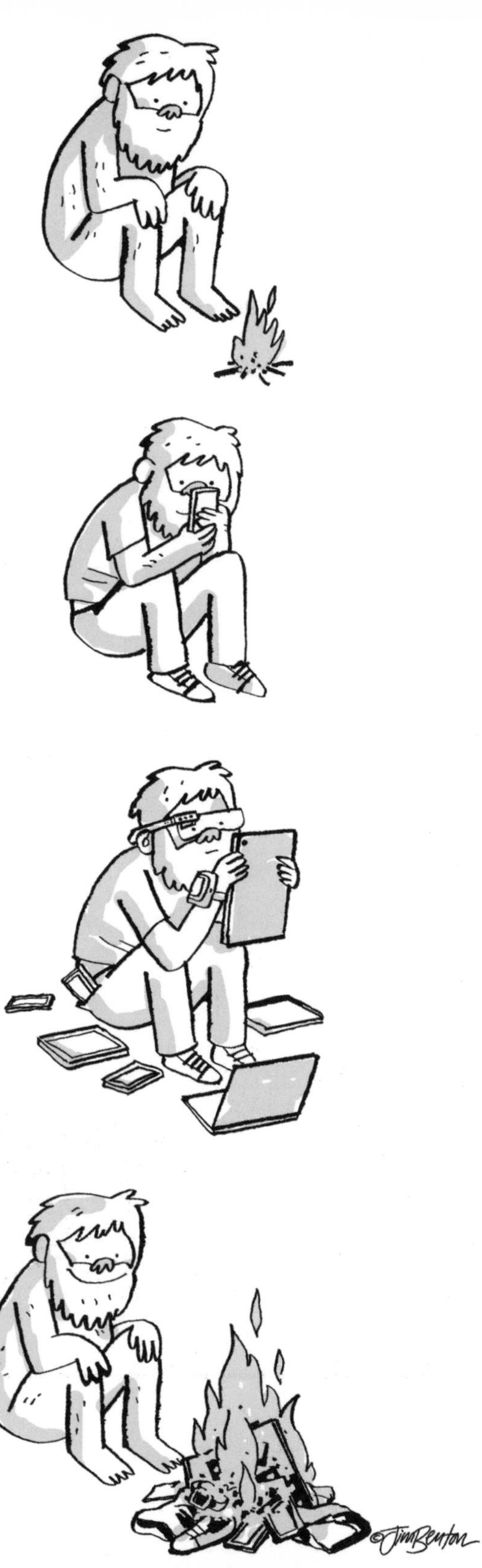
©JimBenton

we should have some kind of totally awesome adventure.
YES! OH MY GOD. THIS IS PERFECT!
©JimBenton

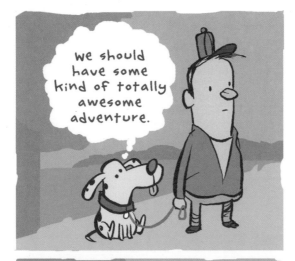

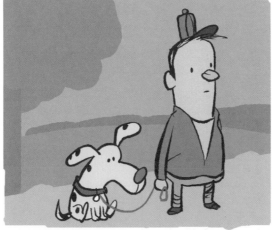

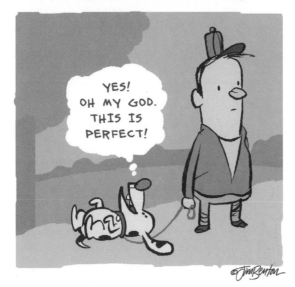

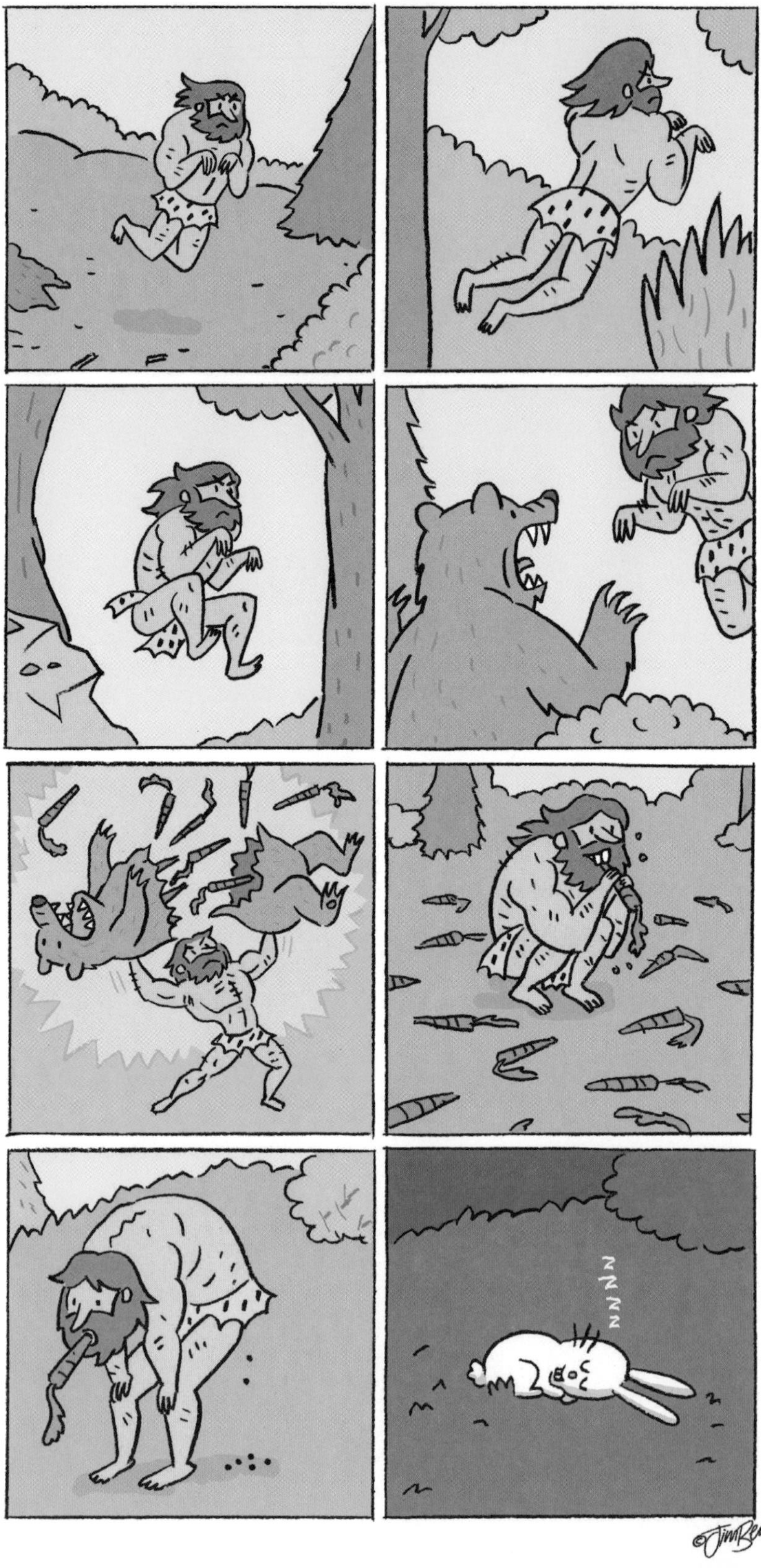

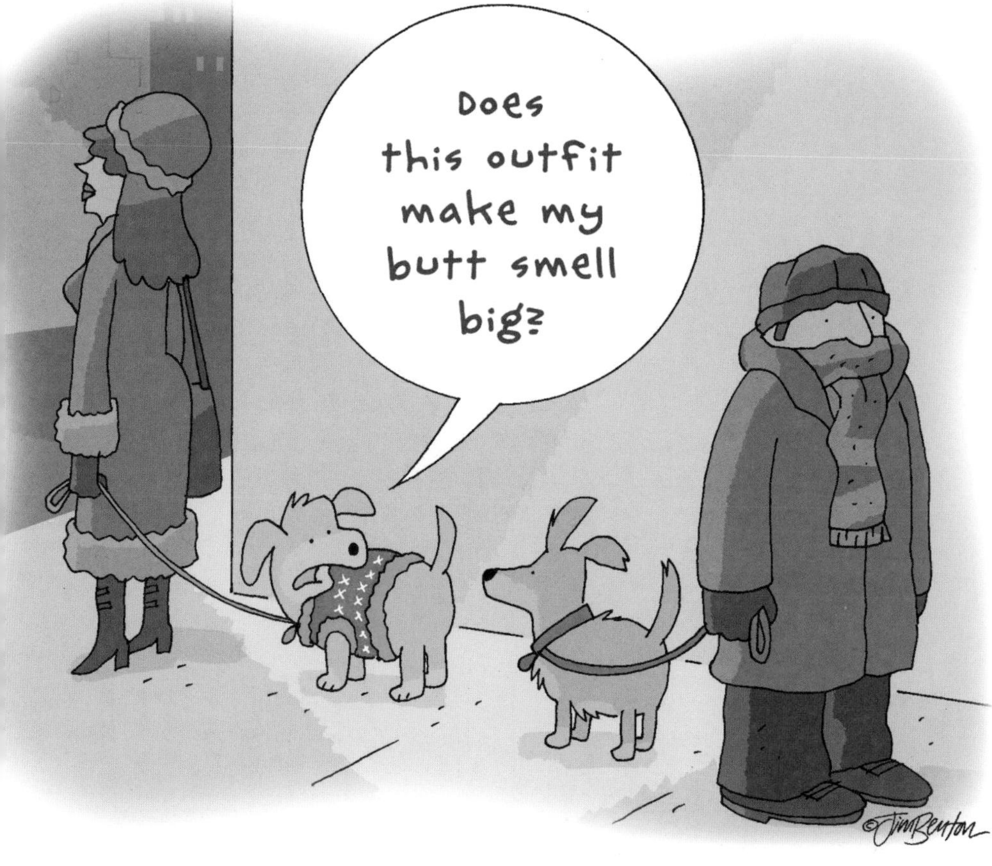
Does this outfit make my butt smell big?
©Jim Benton

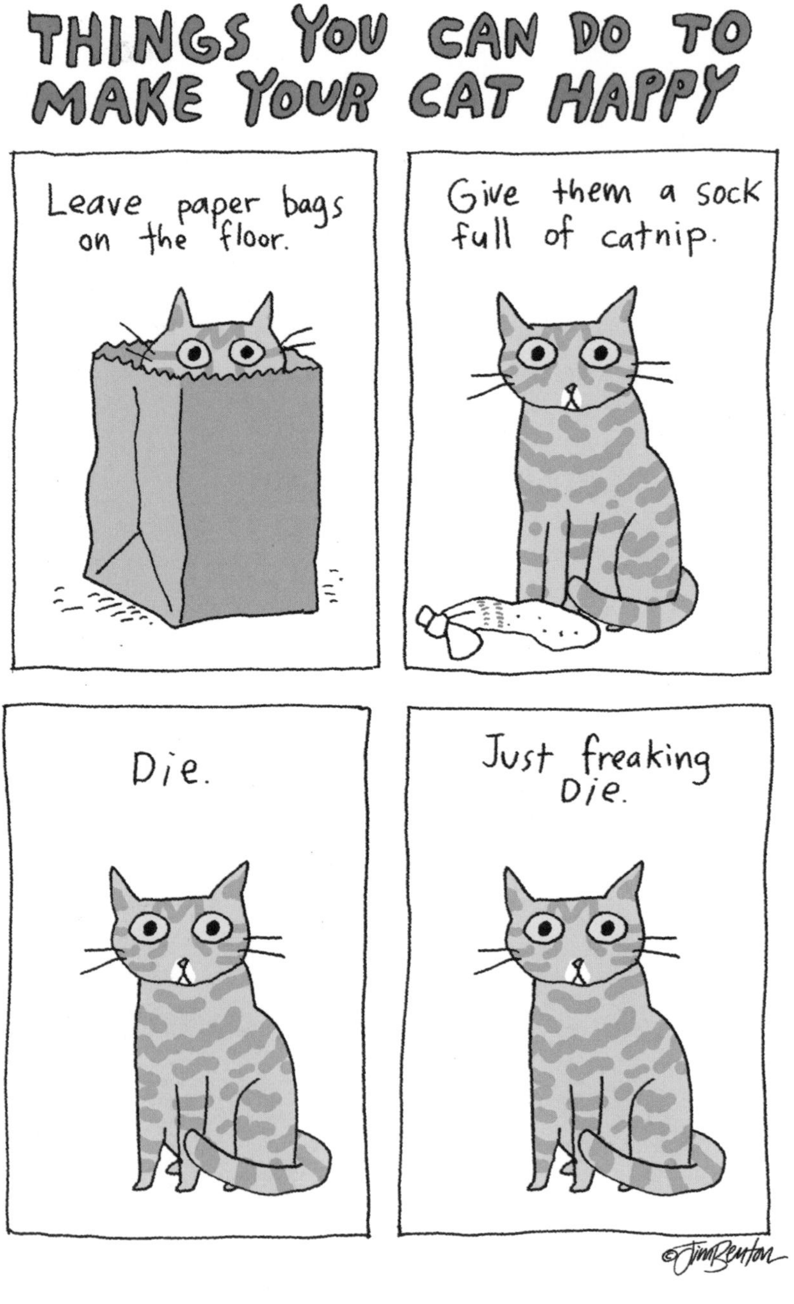
THINGS YOU CAN DO TO MAKE YOUR CAT HAPPY
Leave paper bags on the floor.
Give them a sock full of catnip.
Die.
Just freaking Die.
©Jim Benton

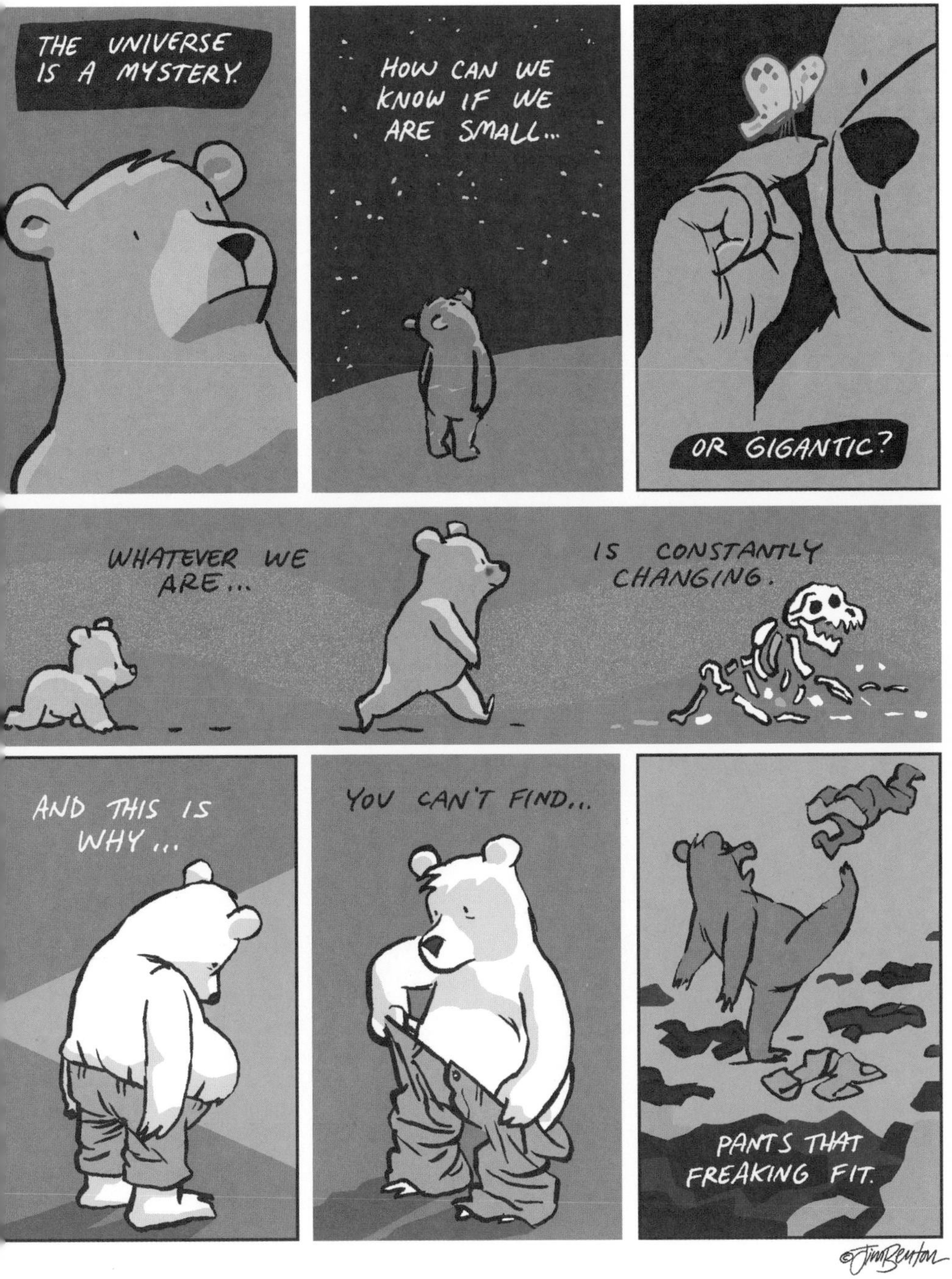
THE UNIVERSE IS A MYSTERY.
HOW CAN WE KNOW IF WE ARE SMALL...
OR GIGANTIC?
WHATEVER WE ARE...
IS CONSTANTLY CHANGING.
AND THIS IS WHY...
YOU CAN'T FIND...
PANTS THAT FREAKING FIT.
©Jim Benton

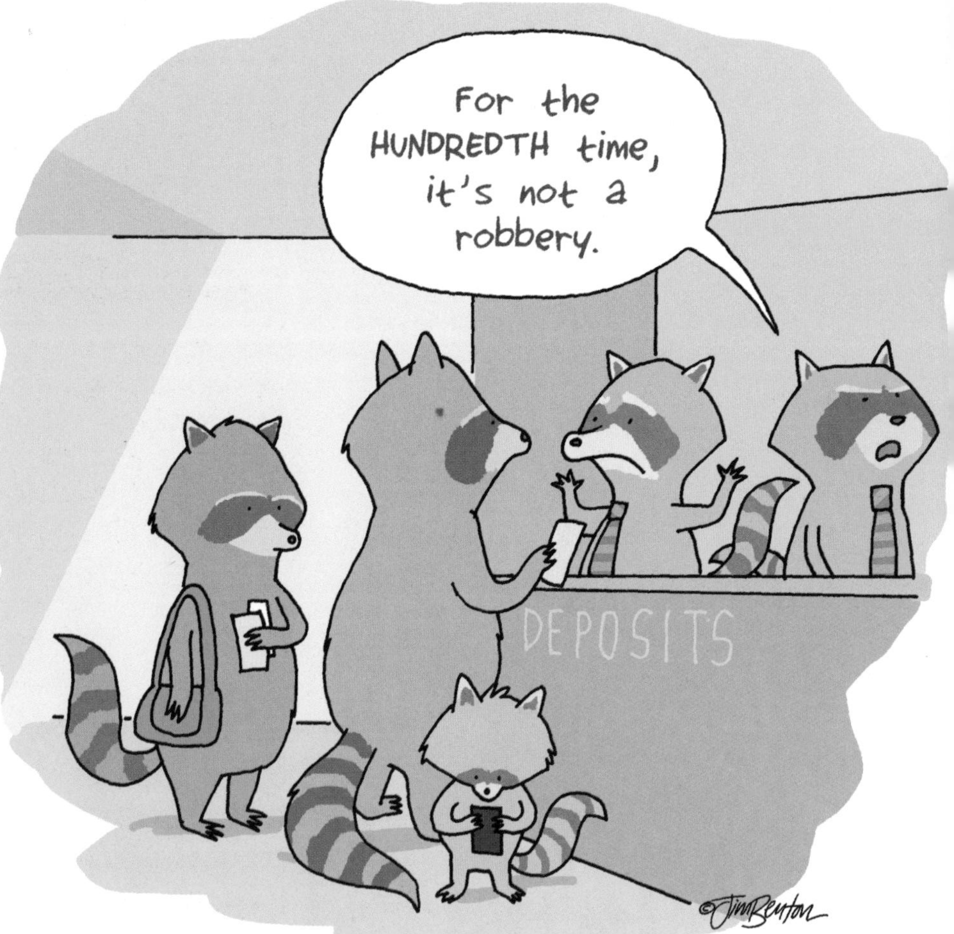
For the HUNDREDTH time, it's not a robbery.
DEPOSITS
©Jim Benton

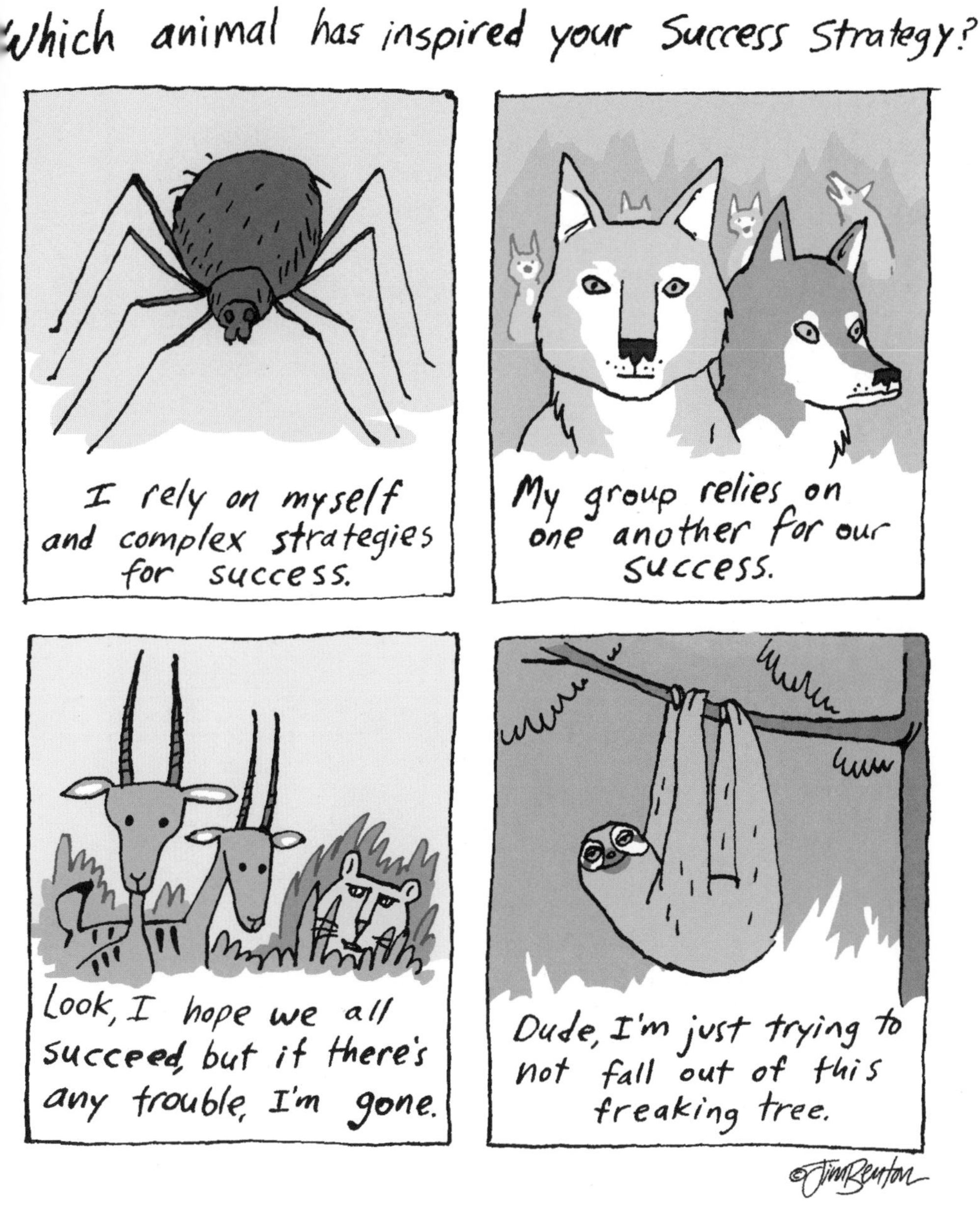
Which animal has inspired your Success Strategy?
I rely on myself and complex strategies for success.
My group relies on one another for our success.
Look, I hope we all succeed, but if there's any trouble, I'm gone.
Dude, I'm just trying to not fall out of this freaking tree.
©Jim Benton

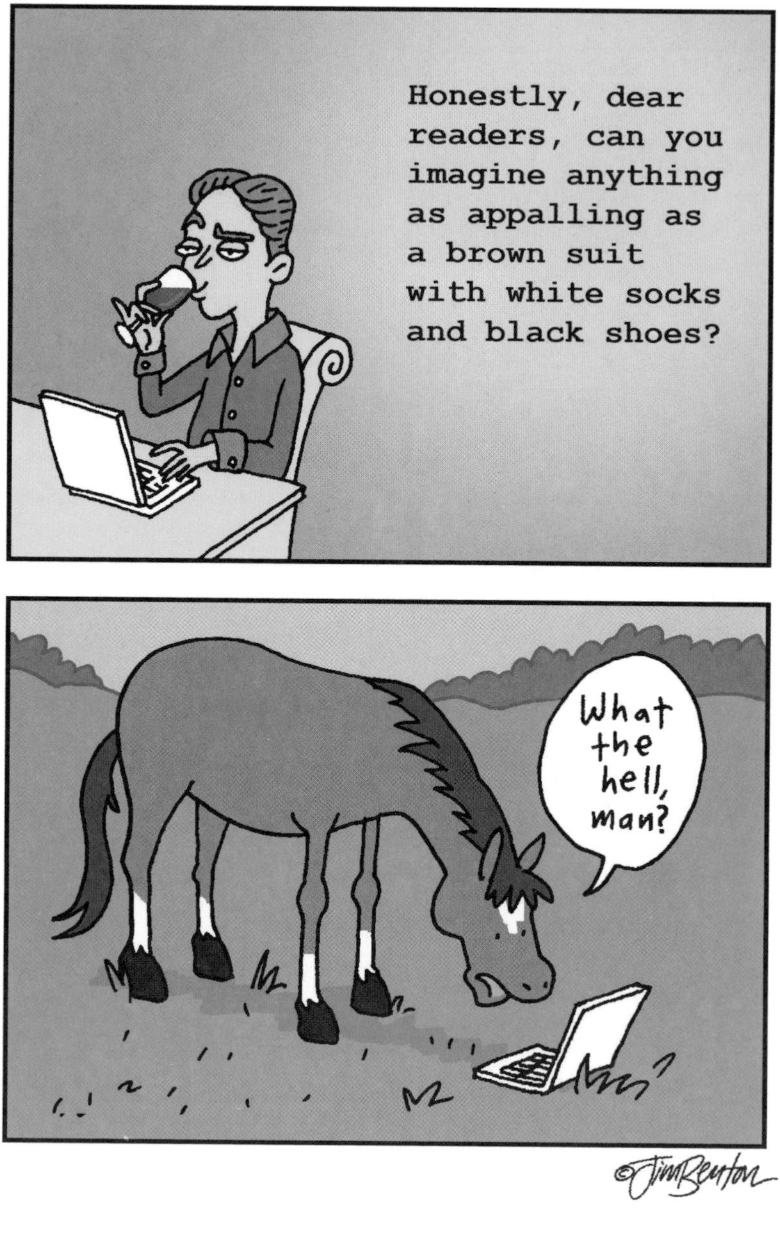
Honestly, dear readers, can you imagine anything as appalling as a brown suit with white socks and black shoes?
What the hell, man?
©Jim Benton

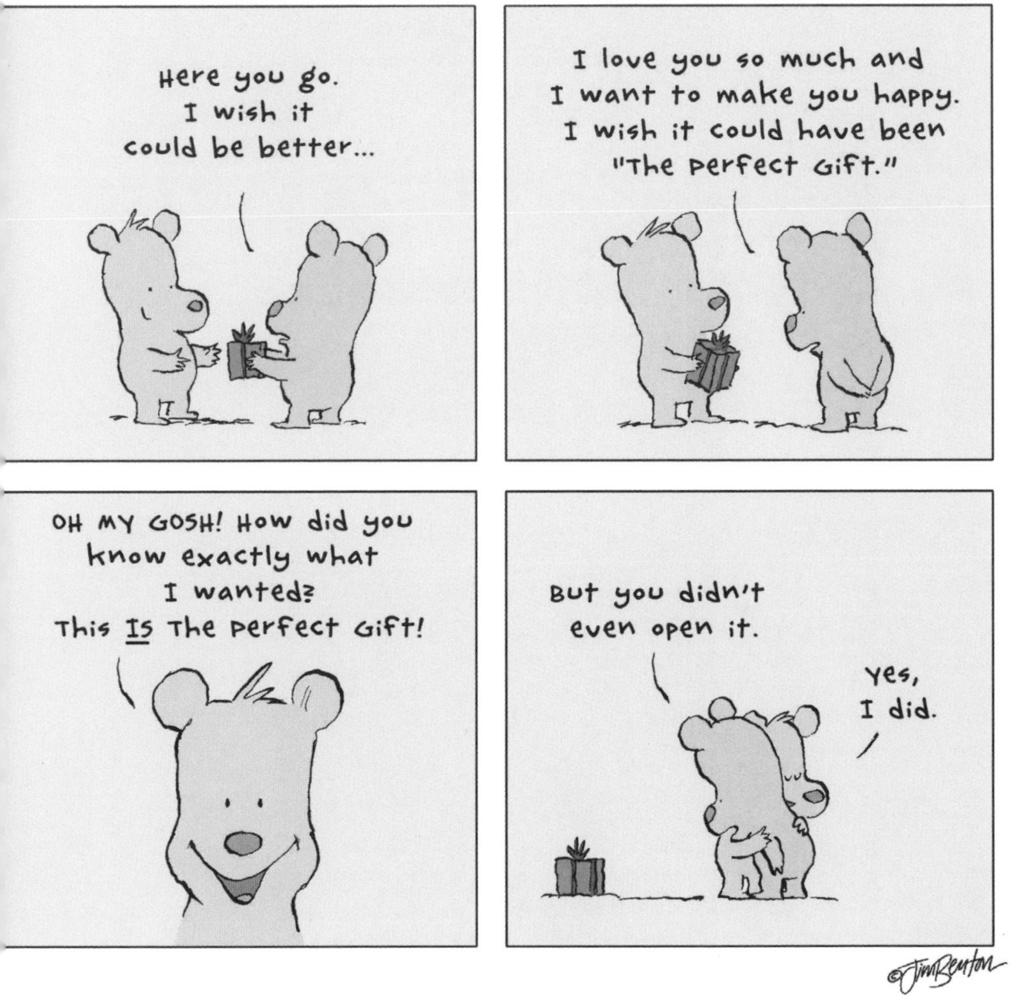
Here you go.
I wish it
could be better...
I love you so much and
I want to make you happy.
I wish it could have been
"The Perfect Gift."
OH MY GOSH! How did you
know exactly what
I wanted?
This IS the Perfect Gift!
But you didn't
even open it.
Yes,
I did.
©Jim Benton

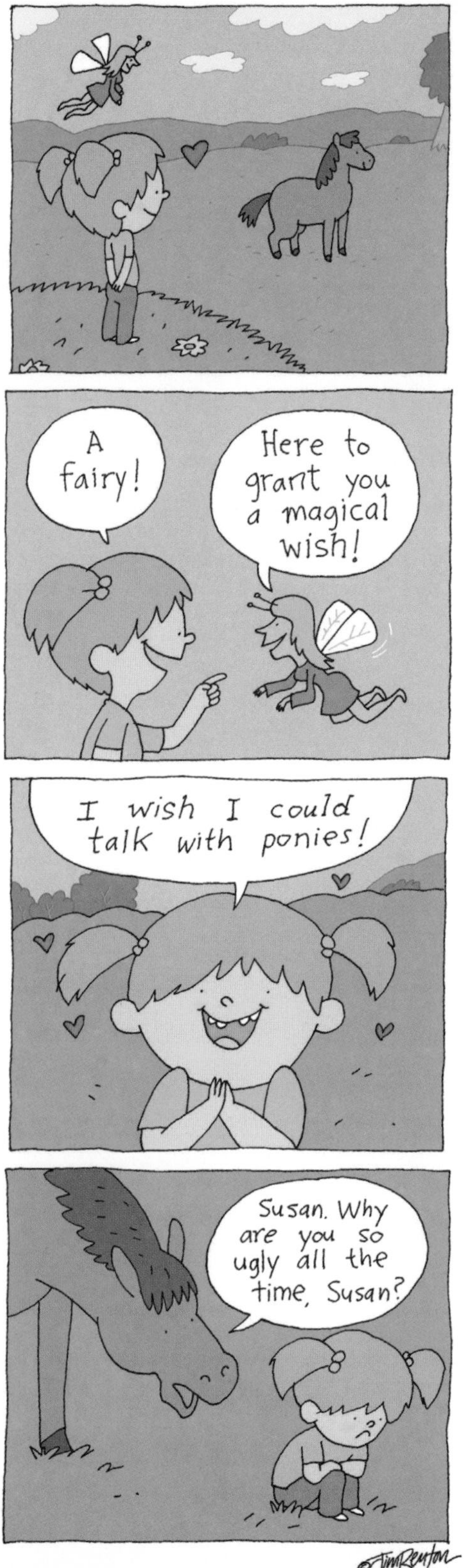
A fairy!
Here to grant you a magical wish!
I wish I could talk with ponies!
Susan. Why are you so ugly all the time, Susan?
©Jim Benton

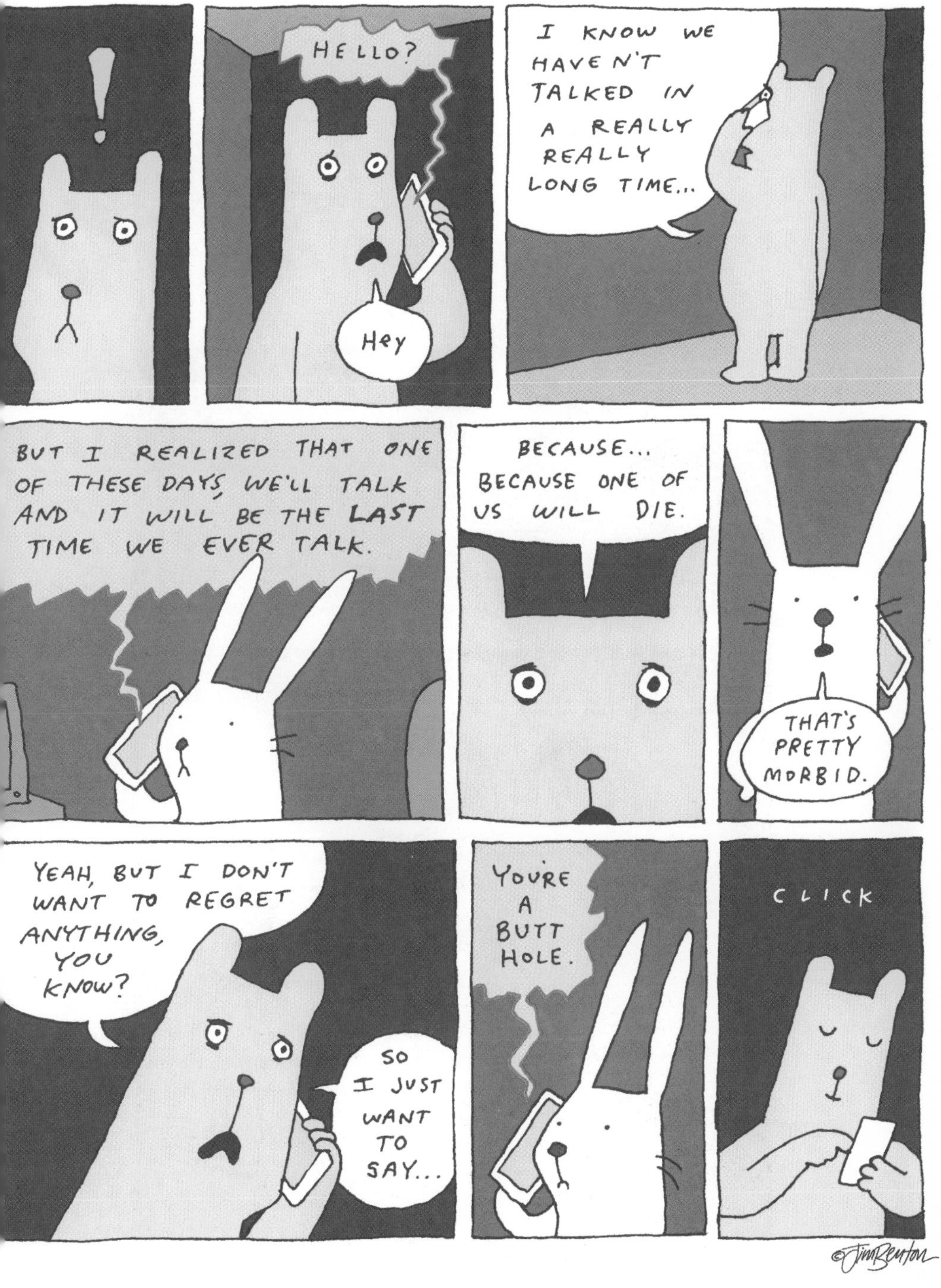
!
HELLO?
Hey
I KNOW WE HAVEN'T TALKED IN A REALLY REALLY LONG TIME...
BUT I REALIZED THAT ONE OF THESE DAYS, WE'LL TALK AND IT WILL BE THE LAST TIME WE EVER TALK.
BECAUSE... BECAUSE ONE OF US WILL DIE.
THAT'S PRETTY MORBID.
YEAH, BUT I DON'T WANT TO REGRET ANYTHING, YOU KNOW?
SO I JUST WANT TO SAY...
YOU'RE A BUTT HOLE.
CLICK
©Jim Benton

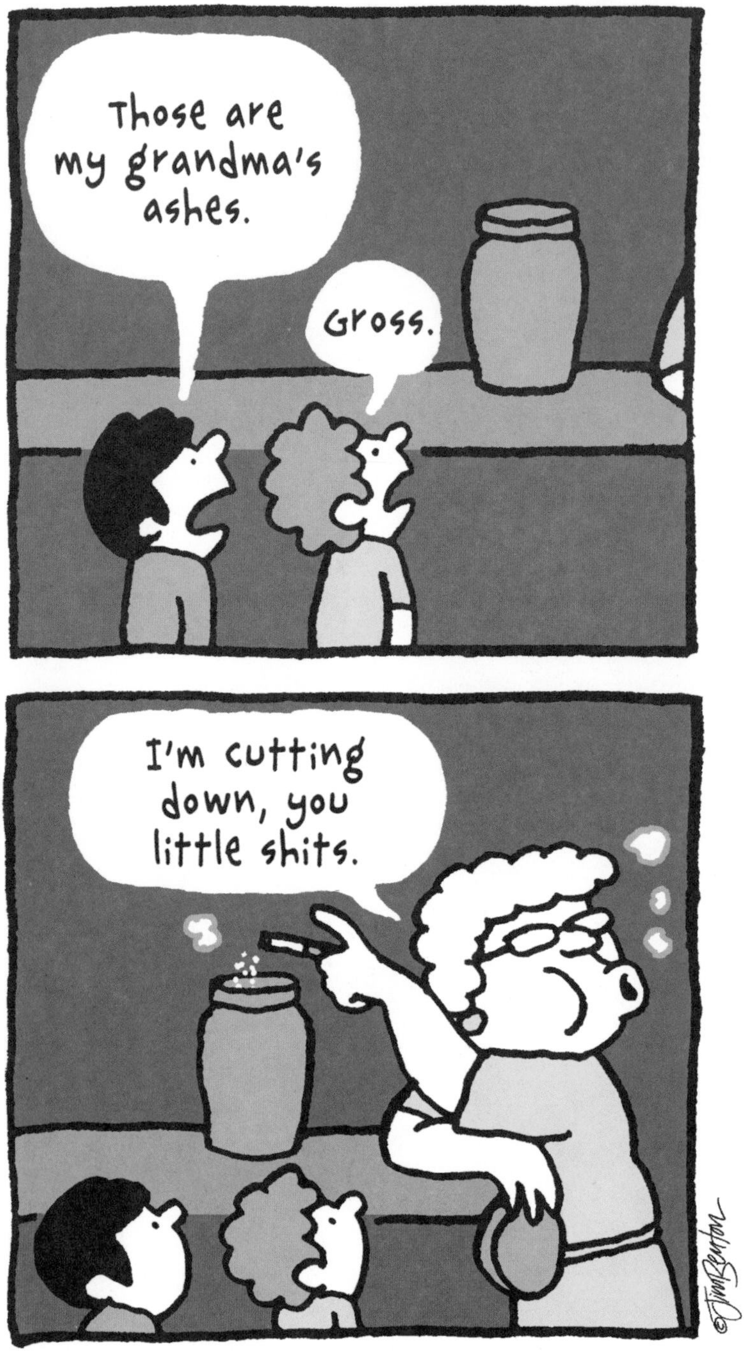
Those are my grandma's ashes.
Gross.
I'm cutting down, you little shits.
©Jim Benton

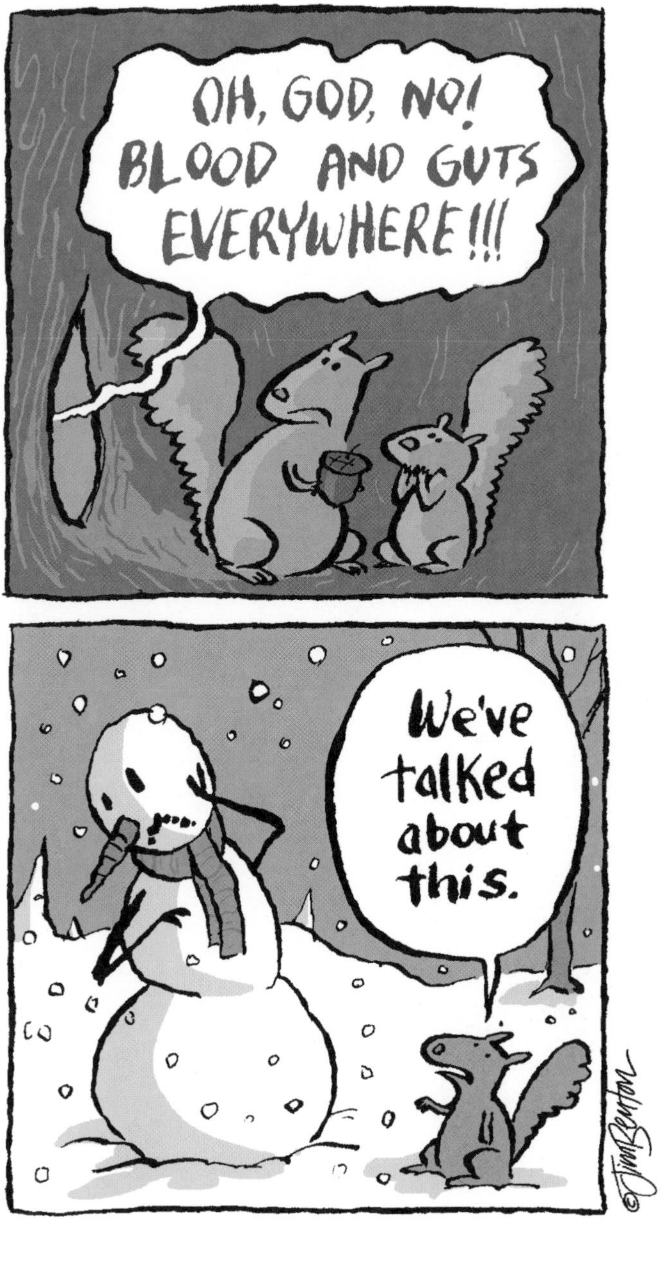
OH, GOD, NO! BLOOD AND GUTS EVERYWHERE!!!
We've talked about this.
©Jim Benton

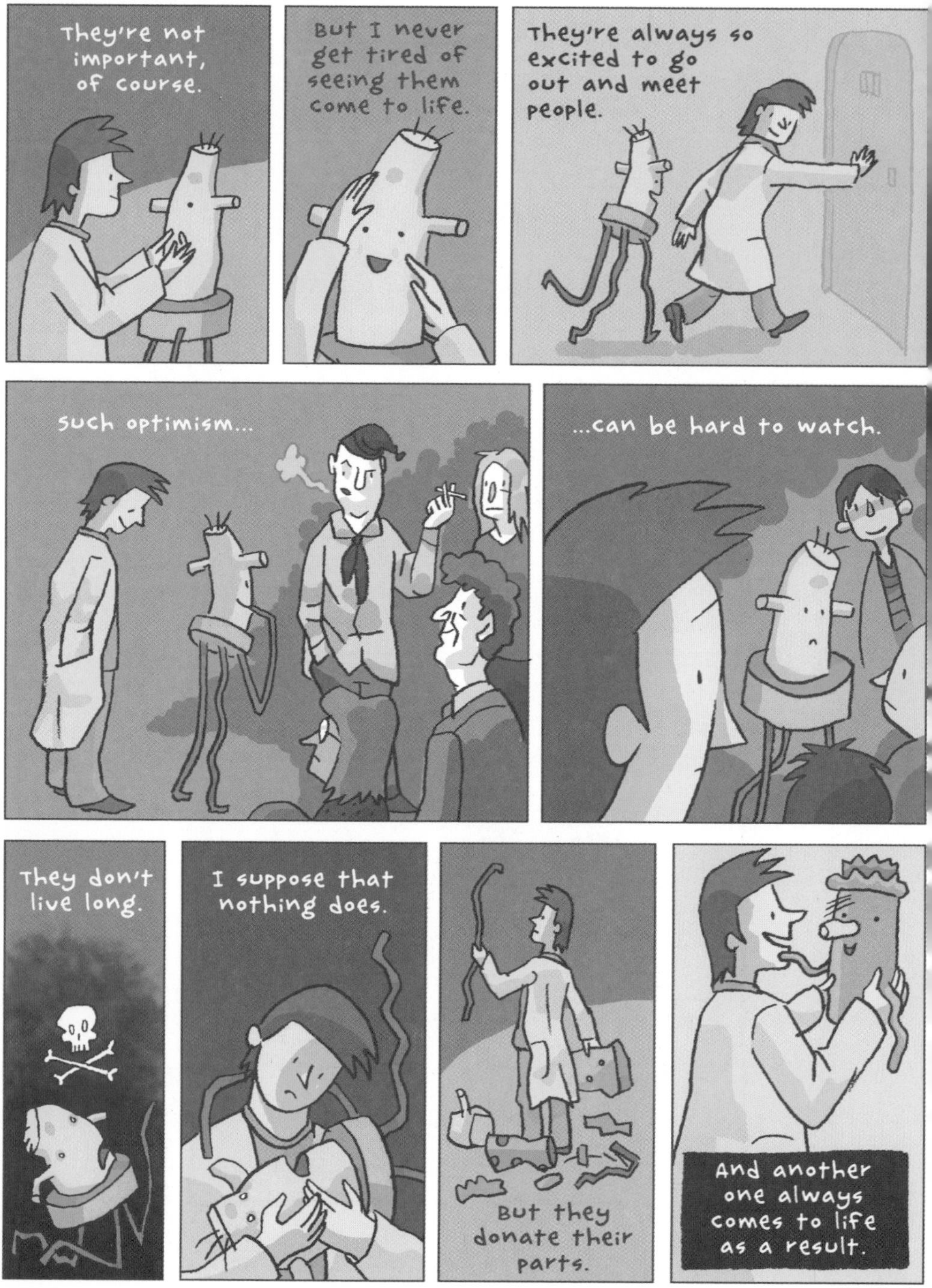
They're not important, of course.
But I never get tired of seeing them come to life.
They're always so excited to go out and meet people.
Such optimism...
...can be hard to watch.
They don't live long.
I suppose that nothing does.
But they donate their parts.
And another one always comes to life as a result.
©Jim Benton

Eternity

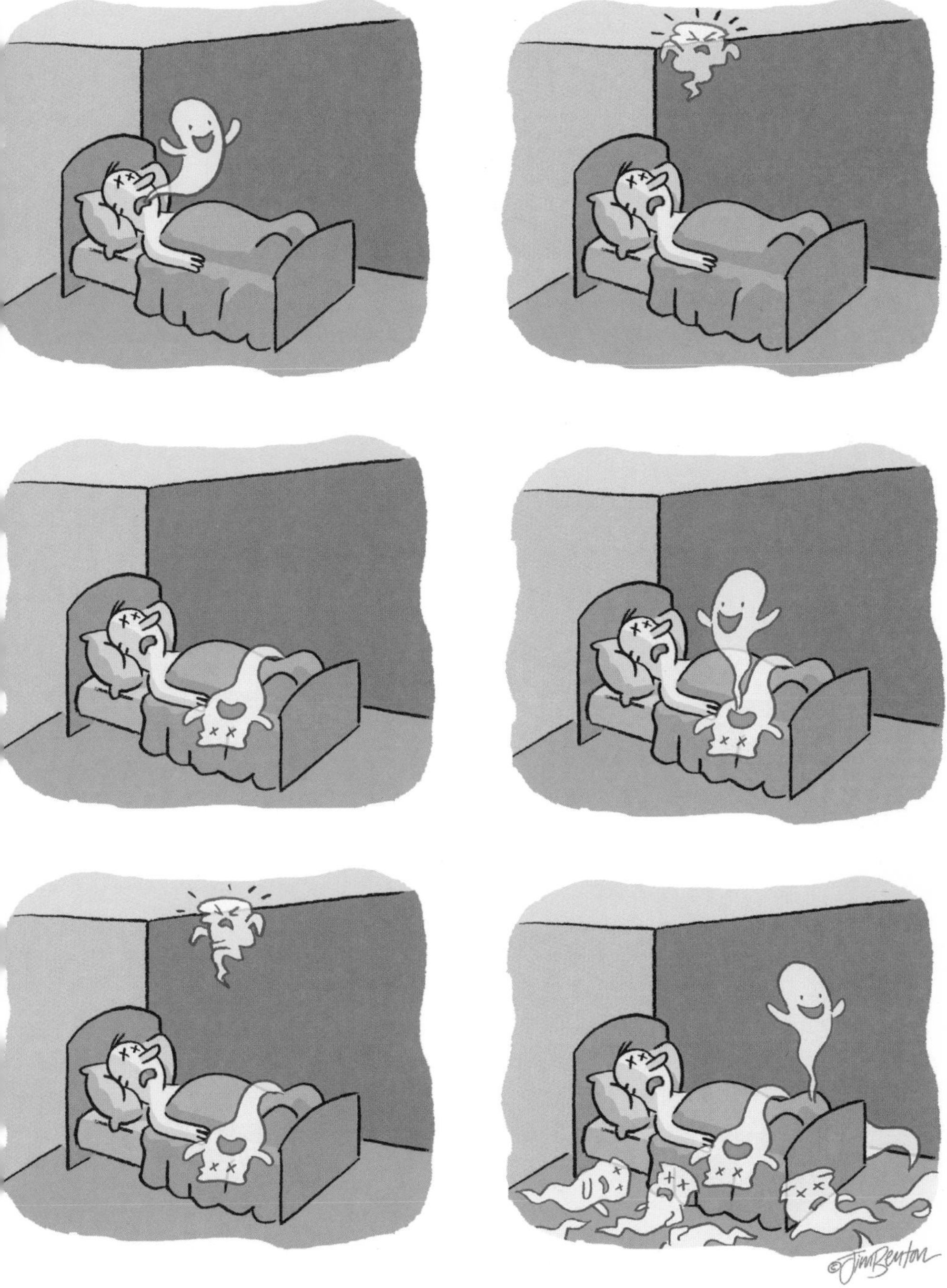
©Jim Benton

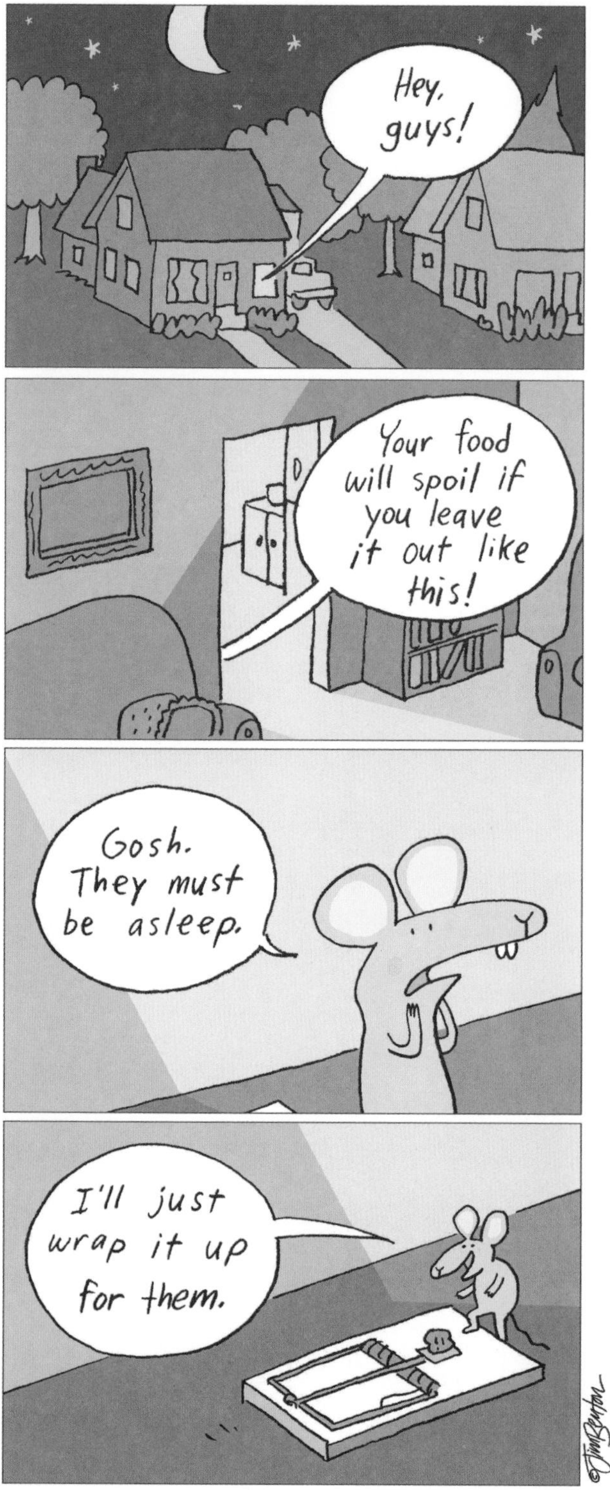
Hey, guys!
Your food will spoil if you leave it out like this!
Gosh. They must be asleep.
I'll just wrap it up for them.

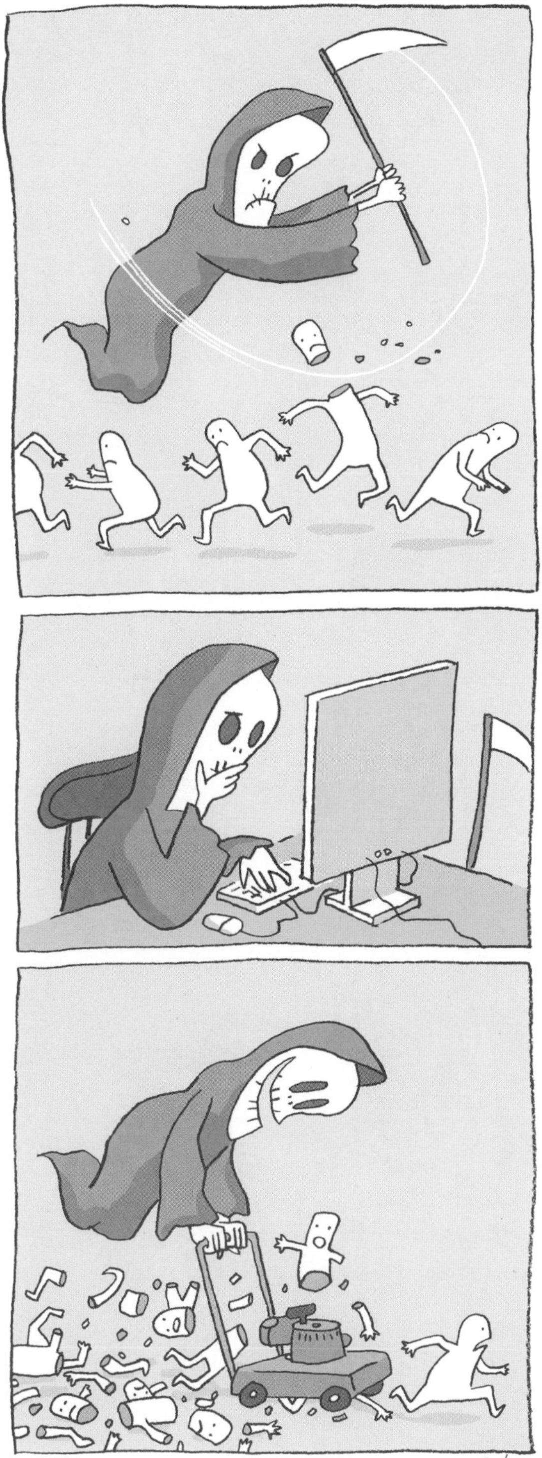
©Jim Benton

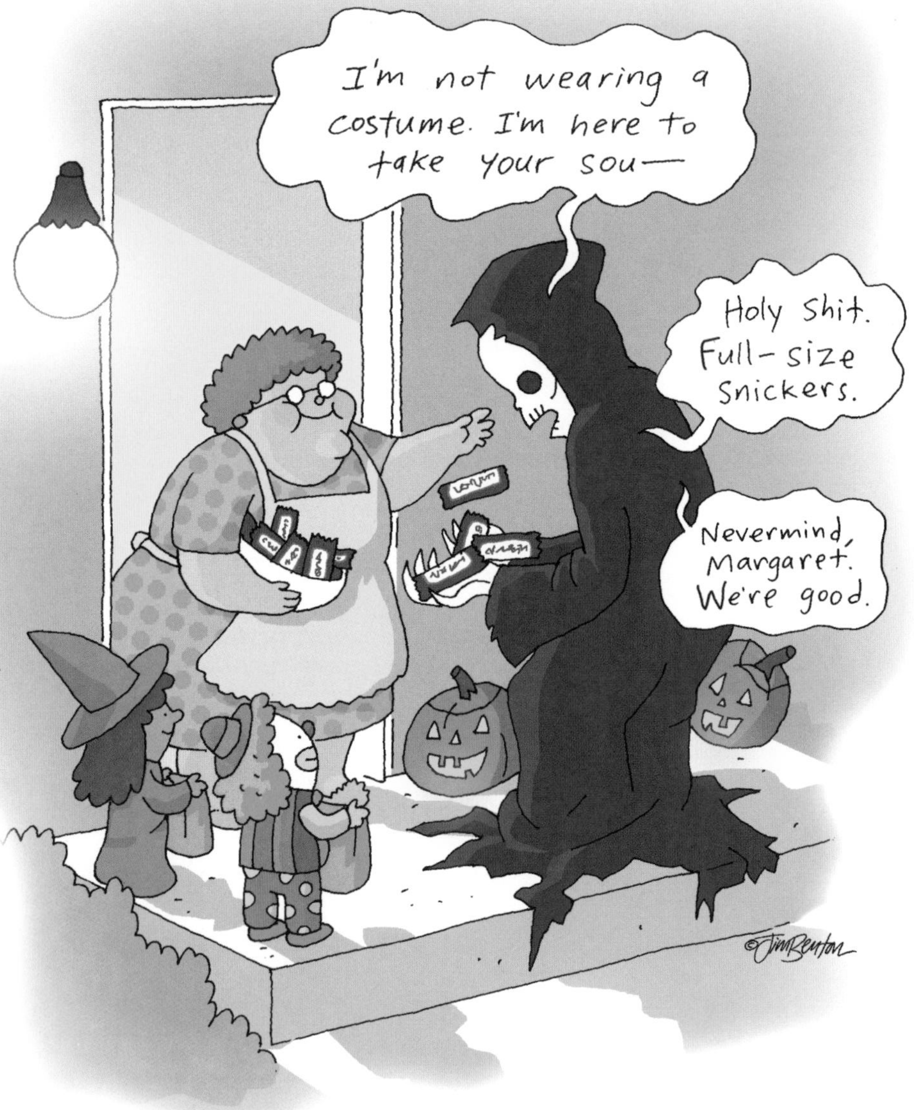
I'm not wearing a costume. I'm here to take your sou—
Holy Shit. Full-size Snickers.
Nevermind, Margaret. We're good.
©Jim Benton

Thanks to Shena Wolf and Kristen LeClerc.

Andrews McMeel Publishing
a division of Andrews McMeel Universal
1130 Walnut Street, Kansas City, Missouri 64106

www.andrewsmcmeel.com

16 17 18 19 20 SDB 10 9 8 7 6 5 4 3 2 1

ISBN: 978-1-4494-7889-6

Library of Congress Control Number: 2016902905

Editor: Shena Wolf
Art Director: Holly Ogden
Production Editor: Maureen Sullivan
Production Manager: Chuck Harper
Demand Planner: Sue Eikos

Attention: Schools and Businesses
Andrews McMeel books are available at quantity discounts with bulk purchase for educational, business, or sales promotional use. For information, please e-mail the Andrews McMeel Publishing Special Sales Department: specialsales@amuniversal.com.